Consider My Servant Job

Consider My Servant Job

Meditations on Life's Struggles and God's Faithfulness

Paul Ciholas

Consider My Servant Job:
Meditations on Life's Struggles and God's Faithfulness

Published by Hendrickson Publishers, Inc.
P.O. Box 3473
Peabody, Massachusetts 01961-3473

Printed in the United States of America.

ISBN 1-56563-372-5

First printing—July 1998

Cover design by Richmond & Williams, Nashville, Tenn.
Interior design by Pilcrow Book Services, Kirkland, Wash.
Edited by Judy Bodmer and Heather Stroobosscher

Detail from
Job Hearing of
His Ruin,
woodcut by
Gustave Doré,
circa 1860

CONTENTS

Introduction 15

Meditation 1 29
There was a man in the land of Uz (Job 1:1)

Meditation 2 34
That man was blameless and upright, one who feared God, and turned away from evil (Job 1:1)

Meditation 3 38
Questionable Success (Job 1:2–5)

Meditation 4 42
"Whence have you come?" (Job 1:7)

Meditation 5 46
"Have you considered my servant Job?" (Job 1:8)

Meditation 6 49
"Does Job fear God for nought?" (Job 1:9)

Meditation 7 54
So Satan went forth from the presence of the LORD. (Job 1:12)

Meditation 8 58
"Naked I came from my mother's womb, and naked shall I return." (Job 1:21)

Meditation 9 62
"You moved me against him, to destroy him without cause." (Job 2:3)

Meditation 10 67
"Curse God, and die." (Job 2:9)

CONTENTS

Meditation 11 71
"Shall we receive good at the hand of God, and shall we not receive evil?" (Job 2:10)

Meditation 12 75
The Day that Should Not Have Been (Job 3)

Meditation 13 80
"Is not your fear of God your confidence,and the integrity of your ways your hope?" (Job 4:6)

Meditation 14 83
"Think now, who that was innocent ever perished? Or where were the upright cut off?" (Job 4:7)

Meditation 15 88
"Can mortal man be righteous before God? Can a man be pure before his Maker?" (Job 4:17)

Meditation 16 91
"Man is born to trouble." (Job 5:7)

Meditation 17 95
"Happy is the man whom God reproves." (Job 5:17)

Meditation 18 98
"Teach me, and I will be silent." (Job 6:24)

Meditation 19 103
"I loathe my life; I would not live forever." (Job 7:16)

Meditation 20 107
"Why have I become a burden to thee?" (Job 7:20)

Meditation 21 111
"Inquire, I pray you, of bygone ages." (Job 8:8)

. . . .

CONTENTS

Meditation 22 116

Contending with God
(Job 9:1–12)

Meditation 23 119

"Though I am innocent, my own mouth would condemn me." (Job 9:20)

Meditation 24 121

"Would that there were an umpire between us." (Job 9:33)

Meditation 25 125

"Let me alone, that I may find a little comfort." (Job 10:20)

Meditation 26 129

"Know then that God exacts of you less than your guilt deserves." (Job 11:6)

Meditation 27 132

"Wisdom is with the aged, and understanding in length of days." (Job 12:12)

Meditation 28 137

"Let me have silence." (Job 13:13)

Meditation 29 141

"Only grant two things . . . withdraw thy hand far from me, and let not dread of thee terrify me." (Job 13:20–21)

Meditation 30 145

"Wilt thou frighten a driven leaf and pursue dry chaff?" (Job 13:25)

Meditation 31 149

"If a man die, shall he live again?" (Job 14:14)

Meditation 32 153

"God puts no trust in his holy ones, and the heavens are not clean in his sight." (Job 15:15)

. . . .

CONTENTS

Meditation 33 156
"God has worn me out."
(Job 16:7)

Meditation 34 159
"O earth, cover not my blood, and let my cry find no resting place." (Job 16:18)

Meditation 35 163
"Since thou hast closed their minds to understanding." (Job 17:4)

Meditation 36 166
"If I look for Sheol as my house . . . where then is my hope?" (Job 17:13–15)

Meditation 37 170
"How long will you hunt for words?"
(Job 18:2)

Meditation 38 173
"Know then that God has put me in the wrong, and closed his net about me." (Job 19:6)

Meditation 39 176
"I know that my Redeemer lives."
(Job 19:25)

Meditation 40 179
"Why do the wicked live, reach old age, and grow mighty in power?" (Job 21:7)

Meditation 41 184
"Agree with God, and be at peace."
(Job 22:21)

Meditation 42 188
"Oh, that I knew where I might find him!"
(Job 23:3)

Meditation 43 191
"I am terrified at his presence."
(Job 23:15)

CONTENTS

Meditation 44 195
"God pays no attention to their prayer."
(Job 24:12)
Meditation 45 200
Bildad's View of Man
(Job 25)
Meditation 46 204
"He . . . hangs the earth upon nothing."
(Job 26:7)
Meditation 47 209
"As long as my breath is in me."
(Job 27:3)
Meditation 48 213
Job's Hymn on Wisdom
(Job 28)
Meditation 49 218
Times to Be Remembered
(Job 29)
Meditation 50 222
The words of Job are ended.
(Job 31:40)
Meditation 51 226
The Anger of Elihu
(Job 32)
Meditation 52 231
"Job speaks without knowledge, his words are without insight." (Job 34:35)
Meditation 53 234
"God is great, and we know him not."
(Job 36:26)
Meditation 54 239
The LORD answered Job out of the whirlwind.
(Job 38:1)

CONTENTS

Meditation 55 243

"Where were you when I laid the foundation of the earth?" (Job 38:4)

Meditation 56 247

"Will you even put me in the wrong? Will you condemn me that you may be justified?" (Job 40:8)

Meditation 57 251

Behemoth and Leviathan (Job 40:15; 41:1)

Meditation 58 254

"I have uttered what I did not understand, things too wonderful for me, which I did not know." (Job 42:3)

Meditation 59 258

The Perils of Friendship (Job 42:7–9)

Meditation 60 263

Epilogue: The New Job (Job 42:10–17)

Detail from *Job and His Friends,* woodcut by Gustave Doré, circa 1860

. . . .

Out of the depths I cry to thee, O Lord!
Lord, hear my voice!
Let thy ears be attentive to the voice of my supplications!
(Psalm 130:1-2)

Religion is what the individual does with his solitariness.
—A. N. Whitehead.

My paten and my chalice are the depth of a soul laid widely open to all the forces which in a moment will rise up from every corner of the earth and converge upon the Spirit. . . . All the things in the world to which this day will bring increase; all those that will diminish; all those too that will die: all of them, Lord, I try to gather into my arms, so as to hold them out to you in offering. This is the material of my sacrifice; the only material you desire . . .

Lord, what is there in suffering that commits me so deeply to you? Why should my wings flutter more joyfully than before when you stretch out nets to imprison me?
—Père Teilhard de Chardin

INTRODUCTION

n Palm Sunday 1994 during the worship service, a tornado destroyed the building of Goshen United Methodist Church in Piedmond, Alabama, killing twenty people and injuring scores of others. The pageantry intended to celebrate the redeeming coming of Christ gave way to cries of grief and despair while the wrath of nature claimed its sacrificial victims. The Reverend Kelly Clem, pastor of the congregation, lost her four-year-old daughter, Hannah, who died in the cataclysm. At that point, Rev. Clem was not ready to answer the question "why." To people around her, who groped for an explanation, she responded, "We do not know why. I do not think that 'why' is the question right now. We just have to help each other through it."

The irony of the moment filled the surviving faithful with a sense of disbelief, or perhaps even absurdity. The congregation had just finished singing "Jehovah Jireh" (The LORD will provide) when the fury of nature sent debris flying as weapons of destruction. The powerless worshipers did not deserve such a fate.

A few days later, at the funeral of Hannah, the officiating pastor told the congregation, "There are people saying 'why did this happen to a church, God's people?' But we say, 'thank God they were a people grounded in God's love.'" A week after the disaster, on Easter morning, two hundred people sat in folding chairs in the parking lot of the ruined church. There was an outpouring of support and spiritual communion. A friend of the church had made the wooden cross behind the improvised pulpit. Four new stained glass windows, sent by a Roman Catholic Church, created the backdrop of the unusual sanctuary. Kelly Clem, still bruised from injuries she had suffered a week before, read the scriptures and told her congregation, "I feel that we are like a symbol of hope right now."

In times of need we turn to faith. In moments of suffering we implore God's consolation. In the face of tragedy we seek God's compassion. Yet we often stand at the door of our religious sanctuaries with empty hearts and minds, wondering at the silence and distance of a God who does not seem to share our sense of grief and urgency. We often encounter God when he no longer makes sense to us, when we contemplate him from beyond what we have grown accustomed to.

Finding God has remained the perennial quest of those who dare approach a mysterious divine presence hidden from our daily burdens and preoccupations. Personally and collectively we no longer feel the need to be elevated above our sphere of immediacy into another region of life far too inscrutable to appeal to our self-designed notions of success. That which cannot be explained or made useful tends to be rejected as contrary to our purpose. Under those circumstances, we lose the ability to remain instruments of God's will. We would rather inform God of our needs in the hope that he will comply with our conceptions of what life ought to be. But God remains beyond what we can say, know, believe, or proclaim about him. To reduce him to anything else may give us an illusory sense of security. With God we always stand at the door of the unknown.

We could envisage Job as a master teacher in church schools or seminaries. His friends give us a list of his credentials, and we feel humble by comparison. He is

. . . .

the image of success, a human being who cared for the people of Uz, for the weak, the poor, the discouraged. He considered himself a father and priest who could atone for the sins of many. He enjoyed numerous favors he considered gifts of God. Yet those alleged blessings were only the fragile manifestations of a life which lacked fulfillment, of a life which had not yet discovered the side of God that lies outside of the common and the usual.

As the result of tragic circumstances and losses, Job's pilgrimage became frightening. It no longer fit a pattern of expected religious behavior. God chose to speak from a whirlwind in the presence of the leviathans of the world, in the midst of a chaos which refused to be subdued by either faith or rational analysis. Job sought refuge in wisdom just to conclude that it could no longer be a part of his new world. In some instances, ritual religion can distance us from God, even when we comply with detailed religious requirements. We discover him in our willingness to stand alone in a quest which fails to be enlightened by friends and teachers. Job bears out the truth of A. N. Whitehead's remark, "Religion is what the individual does with his solitariness."

Our true vocation may be hidden behind the business of a hurried world, and we may be spared a great deal of sorrow by never discovering it. In the face of such a vocation, both Job and Jeremiah wished they had never been born and cursed the day of their birth. The proximity of God may prove overpowering. Our Christian upbringing does not always prepare us for such encounters. Deeply personal, often wrenching encounters with God can be frightening.

Our spiritual thirst keeps us yearning for the unity of all things and for communion with the divine. But

. . . .

we seek in vain for perfection within creation. From tragedy to hope, from despair to faith, from indignation to equanimity, most of us, at one point or another, travel a rocky road fraught with peril, doubt, and suffering. Our canons of justice and fairness provoke in us a sense of indignation when God allows evil to triumph and goodness to be defeated. We live in a universe we proclaim to be God's work, but it is never totally at peace with itself. Collective catastrophes and personal tragedies plague our threatened existence and bind us together. Thus we wonder at the vanity of it all until we force our way to God's presence through faith.

In his poetic vision of creation, William Blake addressed this very issued when he portrayed the divine architect as the *Ancient of Days* who wields the compass of perfect forms by designing the cosmos according to immutable patterns. Yet despite divine perfection as we perceive it and praise it, life on this planet exhibits perplexing proofs that evil forces beyond our control can cause the collapse of the best of our physical, intellectual, moral, and spiritual aspirations.

Blake pursued his probing into the human condition in his *Illustrations of the Book of Job*. His lyric power permeated his masterpiece *The Marriage of Heaven and Hell*, a quest for the interconnectedness of all things at a time when rational explanations fail.

The conflict between divine perfection and human frailty preoccupied the great astronomer Kepler. After years of research and observation, he could establish the laws that govern what appeared to his peers as the puzzling behavior of heavenly bodies. He never ceased to debate, prove, and praise the divine harmony

. . . .

that keeps the celestial orbs in their immutable paths in the heavens. Like Job, Kepler contemplated a God who can hang the earth upon nothing. He marveled at the cosmos and found in it the reflection of the universal mind of a creator whose masterwork would extend into eternity.

Yet everything on earth conspired to keep Kepler and the members of his family in sorrow and distress. Soon after the murder of his best friend, David Fabricius, his most beloved son died of smallpox at the age of six. Then his wife, who was "numbed by the horrors of the soldiers" during the Thirty Years War, died of typhus at an early age. Later, his mother was accused of witchcraft and threatened with torture. She was acquitted by the pleading of her son, who had become the imperial mathematician. She died six months after her release from prison. Kepler then wrote, "Let us despise the barbaric neighings which echo through these noble lands and awaken our understanding and longing for the harmonies." He lost everything, including his precious life when, poor and destitute, he succumbed to illness. Kepler had written his own epitaph: "I measured the skies, now I measure the shadows. Skybound was the mind, the body rests in the earth."

Like Kepler we often feel inclined to shed tears at the thought that, in spite of divine perfection, most of us will encounter suffering and discouragement in our pilgrimage through life.

The Book of Job surges into our consciousness as a divinely ordered challenge. Every time we have cause to question the proper functioning of creation as we experience it in our daily lives, the Book of Job realigns our perspective on God's providence.

Through the first eight years of his life, my oldest son was nearsighted, but my wife and I did not know it. He memorized eye-tests at school, because he knew it wasn't good to fail. He adapted adroitly to his view of the world. One day, while in our company, he mistook a pile of rubbish for his friends. So we drove him straight to the optometrist's office. His next few weeks were filled with awe and wonder. This experience brought home the truth that we need correct vision to bring our world into focus.

The Book of Job refocuses our vision when life becomes a blur of incomprehensible events. Even with the sharpest insight we are not able to perceive God in his majesty. But in our darkest moments we can turn to Job to gain new perspective. While in the depths of tribulation he refused to exclude from human affairs a God he could no longer comprehend.

In our quest for righteous living, we keep alive in our souls the moral and spiritual qualities which do not disappear when we feel abandoned by God. Often in life we have to depend on ourselves to create the inner equilibrium which testifies to our resilience, to the presence of divine gifts which keep us from error even when we fail to acknowledge them.

Through suffering we journey to the peace which passes all understanding and forge the links of a chain which become the visible symbols of our common bond of humanity. In solitariness we gain our spiritual vision, as we contemplate our place within a divine purpose not always discernible to us when our hearts and minds are subjected to the tumult of a world adrift in stormy seas. In solitude we acquire the wisdom which helps us distinguish between that which can be grasped by the mind and that which must remain within the realm of faith and mystery.

Job teaches us there is a spiritual part of ourselves which cannot be destroyed by the wounds inflicted on

. . . .

us, however seriously they may injure us. This lesson is difficult to learn, for inner resonance must be achieved on a personal level, often in opposition to the seemingly rational order of our environment.

Throughout the ages the universal voice of humankind reminds us of scenes of solitariness in the never-ending quest for redemption. Religion and literature offer many examples of suffering and solitariness which have symbolized our perennial plight: Prometheus nailed to his rock, Mohammed retreating to his wilderness, Buddha absorbed in his meditations, Orpheus losing what he had been able to rescue from Hades, Job on his dung heap, and Christ on the cross, crying to God, "Why hast thou forsaken me?"

Aeschylus has Agamemnon proclaim, "God, whose will has marked for man the sole way where wisdom lies; ordered one eternal plan: Man must suffer to be wise."

Job's friends believed that we are endowed with the ability to know the source and reason of our tribulations and chastisements. But in reality we fail to pursue wisdom when our knowledge finds itself at odds with the great mysteries of life and when we feel trapped in a web which seems indifferent to our presence in it. When we reduce everything to our myopic viewpoints, we frustrate ourselves and the creator who placed in us the ability to discern the higher from the lower.

As vulnerable pawns in an uncertain destiny, we persist in confusion, exchanging the better for the worse while believing that we follow God's will. Thus Goethe spoke of "the dangerous gift from above," as it is easily misconstrued and misapplied when disconnected from its source. Job found no communion of spirit with his well-meaning friends, and Christ found that those who should ensure peace on earth can occasionally weave crowns of thorns.

At points Job rebelled against a one-way relationship in the universe of divine dominion. But humanity is bound to live under the eternal law of the creator without having the privilege to alter it. What we are and what we do never amounts to what is ultimately expected of us. In our earthly existence our standards and canons of moral and intellectual rectitude are not automatically linked together by universal decrees that would give us the proper scales on which to weigh our joys and sorrows. God and Satan finalized the terms of the wager with full disregard for Job's possible objections. Similarly, we are called upon to play our part in a drama whose script we did not write.

Falsely accused of treason against the state, and unjustly condemned to spend the last years of his life in a prison cell, the sixth-century Roman philosopher Boethius bitterly complained that it is nothing short of monstrous that God should look on while the forces of evil are allowed to achieve their purpose against righteous and innocent people.

Job, who for a long time in his life was brought up on the milk of learning and on the honey of success, was reduced to seeing his life unfold as if watching a cosmic film that failed to develop properly, projecting image after image without forming a coherent picture. Only in an act of confidence and faith did he come to accept the contradictions and paradoxes that filled his life, and this to the dismay of those who had always considered him a righteous and virtuous person.

In the perspective of temporal existence, Job would have fared better if he had been ignored by God. Instead he was cast into the role of the long-suffering servant.

. . . .

Job's desperate prayer confirms that feeling: "Let me alone that I may find some comfort." Divine presence does not always ensure blessings according to our human expectations.

The Book of Job teaches us that we contemplate life only from a limited perspective. Somewhere in the depths of infinity lies a buried part of ourselves: that something we did not bring with us into this life, the missing piece which makes us incomplete and generates in us the yearning to be connected again with the source of our being, beyond our distorted view of perfection and innocence. But what we do not remember, we cannot recover, for it must remain surrounded by the eternal silence of a mystery unspoken forever, though very real within divine providence. Incompleteness inexorably belongs to life. The yearning to overcome it ennobles our human vocation.

Sometimes, like Job, in an act of faith, we must allow ourselves to believe God has rescued a corner of his creation that does not partake of the absurdity of the rest. Then it is up to the poet, to the prophet, to the saint to help us escape from the hopelessness that imprisons us in our transient world. Now that we carry within ourselves the burden of mortality, our eyes can see no further than the immediate, as they belong to a body that is itself threatened by its own deficiencies. Somehow to appear in this world is to lose the depth of being. Even Christ knew this. In the deepest moments of his agony, he prayed God to glorify him again with the glory he had before the world was made. The existence of the physical world accentuates the power of evil and makes redemption more difficult.

The Book of Job is a revolt against the facile solution.

. . . .

The realm of redemption is not a realm of escape but an invitation to participate in the divine act of creation. Job understood that every gift in life is a gift from God. But at the same time Job also knew that nothing is ever completely ours. In truth, we are only guests in God's kingdom and err when we forget that fundamental relationship to our creator. *Sic transit gloria mundi.* A century before the time of Christ the non-conformist Roman poet Lucretius wrote, "Life's a gift to no man, only a loan to him. Look back at time. How meaningless, how unreal!" Indeed, only the end will finally enlighten a process that we so desperately attempt to enter and control.

In the perspective of eternity, we do not fully understand God's purpose which contained each of us before the world came into being. In our earthly journey, we must accept the painful proposition that what sustains our lives can also cause our death. It may shock our moral sensitivity that God would deal with the sons of evil and Satan on what appears to be an equal level of purpose. In the case of Job, the heavenly powers project the image of a divine family sharing the same wagers afflicting creation.

Becoming like God meant knowing both good and evil. The Book of Genesis does not shy away from universalizing the dominion of good and evil as the negative bond uniting mortals and God. Satan reassures Eve that the end of knowledge is not death, but similarity with God: "Your eyes will be open, and you will be like God, knowing good and evil." Later the heavenly powers agree: "Behold, the man has become like one of us, knowing good and evil." The closer we come to God in our attempt to be true to our vocation, the more we realize we cannot be spared from evil in order to participate in good.

. . . .

Job's story converges upon the limits of the rationally possible. He must acknowledge the disintegration of all things around him while proclaiming the wholeness of God. From the devastation of the moment he must rise to an eschatological consciousness that can transcend judgment, despair, and even death. In that process he learns that there is in suffering a mysterious force which manifests the very presence of God among us.

Some of our modern Jobs, such as Elie Wiesel and Viktor Frankl, experienced the cruelty and absurdity of the world to a degree rarely surpassed. It was from the confines of a concentration camp that Viktor Frankl wrote, "If there is a meaning in life at all, then there must be a meaning in suffering. Suffering is an ineradicable part of life, even as fate and death. Without suffering and death human life cannot be complete."

The existence of suffering raises the question of divine fairness and justice. Nature dispenses its goodness on all, but it can also strike indiscriminately through storms, earthquakes, floods, illness, death, and other forms of physical and mental distress. The hope for universal harmony is the most elusive quest of the human race. Successful life and divine favor do not mix, for we come closer to God in suffering and tragedy than in comfort and affluence. In the case of Job, the harmony between prosperous life and divine endorsement must be broken to test the faithfulness of a person who traditionally associates well-being with divine approval.

Faith is what remains after we lose everything else.

Faith is consequently very rare and totally escapes the purview of Job's wife and friends. Beyond the trappings of religious rituals, we learn with great difficulty how to worship God rather than our conception of him. It is precisely those who are already grounded in their faith who can begin the most meaningful search for a key to the mystery and inscrutability of God. The rebellion of Job is more acceptable to God than the complacency of his friends. Divine blessings are not subject to proofs, and they often come to us clothed in strange garments.

There is little need to stress the literary and spiritual beauty, poignancy, and influence of the Book of Job. The faith of millions of people is vicariously symbolized in its perennial appeal, giving a human face to tragedies that might otherwise remain unbearable. We shall never be able to understand why the just suffer and the evil prosper for the simple reason that our human calculations are not part of divine mathematics. We must learn how to live as incomplete beings in an unfinished universe. We see God's process from the middle, not the end.

The God of immanence cannot be grasped apart from a transcendence which keeps him hidden from us and saves us from the absurdity of certain claims to knowledge and special divine favors. Perhaps Teilhard de Chardin said it best: "In its present state the world would be unintelligible, and the presence in it of reflection would be incomprehensible, unless we supposed there be a secret complicity between the infinite and the infinitesimal to warm, nourish and sustain to the very end. . . . *Man is irreplaceable.* Therefore, however improbable it might seem, *he must reach the goal,* not necessarily, doubtless, but infallibly."

It is that kind of complicity between the heavenly and the earthly that we do not always understand in the Book of Job. If we did, we might also find that in spite of anger and frustration, the message is reassuring and peaceful, though not according to the standards we commonly apply to everyday events in life.

. . . .

In the Book of Job, we come face to face with a most profound religious intuition, with a faith which does not need any proof but itself, with an outlook on divine creation and providence no longer dependent on our losses and sorrows, however tragic they may be, and with a God whose majesty far surpasses the vulgarities of praise and power. Job's friends had to vindicate what they believed to be the unalterable divine rule of rewards and punishments. Against his will Job had to learn at great cost that, as Whitehead pointed out, "In considering religion, we should not be obsessed by the idea of its necessary goodness. This is a dangerous delusion."

Long before Christ asserted his belief in a small remnant, Job knew what was meant by the wisdom of the saying, "Enter by the narrow gate; for the gate is wide and the way is easy, that leads to destruction, and those who enter by it are many. For the gate is narrow and the way is hard, that leads to life, and those who find it are few." Job did not deliberately choose the narrow way. It was never truly visible to him, though real beyond expression. God must have appeared strange in the midst of ashes, proclaimed by a servant full of sores. To surviving worshipers whose palm fronds of hope were crushed in nature's fury, God must have seemed terribly distant and perhaps even cruel. Those who died under the collapsed walls of Goshen United Methodist church as well as the thousands of daily victims of all kinds of tragedies compel us to wonder about the wagers made in heaven and about our ignorance of divine purpose.

The story of Job is vast enough to contain the questions for which we do not find answers. It invites us to let our thoughts flow without the fear of being wrong, but with the conviction that, somewhere within eternity, when we shall see face to face and no longer through a glass darkly, we shall understand why "the sufferings of the present time are not worth comparing with the glory that is to be revealed to us."

Detail: servant from *Job Hearing of His Ruin,* woodcut by Gustave Doré, circa 1860

MEDITATION 1.

There was a man in the land of Uz. (Job 1:1)

n the beginning the spirit of God was moving over the elements of creation, and in that spirit, the source of all new being, were already inscribed the names of those who would journey with the creator through the mysteries of earthly existence. In the book of life, some names were printed in bold characters. They were refused the privilege of anonymity in view of a special vocation whose terms were dictated by God. Their destiny was marked by heavenly decisions. They did not choose the road to travel, nor did they know of the dangers they would encounter on it. They would have to pay the price of suffering for the persistence of tragic and mortal flaws among their contemporaries, and, in most unexpected ways, they would bring blessing and redemption to the ever-growing and complex life east of Eden.

"There was a man in the land of Uz." Indeed there were numerous men and women in that land. The statement could be repeated millions of times. There was a woman, there was a man, there was a child anywhere in the land of the living, lost in the vast generations of God's people. And then a name sets apart a unique person in the midst of special circumstances: "There was a man in the land of Uz, whose name was Job," a name destined to have a special meaning within divine purpose and to remain in a prominent place within human memory. At a pace that appeared ruthless, he had to travel the road which led from comfortable anonymity to oppressive identity. He was singled out to know the plight of a person in whom the sons of God and God himself took interest. Job possessed something the heavenly powers covet: his heart, his loyalty, his reciprocal relationships. To be human is to become the battleground upon which heavenly powers try to secure our recognition of their divine majesty and dominion.

Job knew nothing of the deals made in heaven. Like him, we are fated to remain ignorant. We are not privileged to be taken into the secrets of heavenly councils. Without the support of absolute standards, we must guess at what makes life either fruitful or unbearable. The land of the living thrives with the questions and frustrations of the hearts and intellects of millions who attempt to penetrate forbidden secrets.

Job was not different from any of us. His canons of good and evil happened to be right. Ours may be wrong. In his new predicament he was, so to speak, condemned to know good and evil. In the absence of a clear knowledge of divine intentions, he had to find within himself the standards of proper behavior. The silence of God must be met by the wisdom of solitude. Even the counsel of friends was of no avail. In Job God tested his creation. Did he succeed in implanting in the heart and mind of his creature enough resilience to withstand the flaws of a world deprived of momentary perfection? What exactly did God intend to find out in the testing of Job? Was it Job's strength and moral rectitude? Or was God testing the very foundations of his creation?

There are within the absurdity of human events those who are marked for a destiny they could neither foresee nor influence. I will never forget the troubled

. . . .

times of World War II when the Nazis selected my hometown in France for the building of stalags for hundreds of Russian prisoners. I was born into a family of refugees from Slavic lands, so we shared with those unfortunate people a common ethnic background. Both parents and children in my family spoke Russian. After many attempts made by several pastors, the German authorities allowed a group of prisoners to leave the stalags on Sundays to come to my home for religious services. It seemed nothing short of a miracle that the Nazis would let them out. More miraculous during those war years was the fact that my mother's gardening skills yielded enough food not only to feed her family of seven children, but also for a nourishing stew to satisfy the hunger of forty prisoners every Sunday for almost two years.

We soon learned how tragedy can remold people's lives. There was Pyotr, a farmer who lost all of his material possessions and exchanged his last horse for a Bible. There was Ivan, the youngest of them, who had never known his parents. There was Daniel, who suffered greatly for the affirmation of his faith in Stalinistic Russia. There was Boris, the lone survivor of his family killed in the steppes on the Eastern front. There were many others, with different stories, yet the same faith. They had lost everything. There have been many men in the land of Uz.

We met together for the last time on Easter 1944. In a world emptied of everything else, only faith in the resurrection allowed us to speak of hopes and joys which could erase the memory of misery and destitution. Like the friends of Job, we often failed to find the right words to alleviate sorrows belonging to a world that seemed to escape all norms of rationality. After D-Day, the stalags were emptied. Silence prevailed for several weeks. Word came to us that in the disarray a few were able to escape.

. . . .

We heard that most of them were executed. We ourselves survived the ravages of war amid the rubble of ruined cities, but our world was emptied of blessings and friends we considered special gifts of God. I knew then, as never before, that suffering was our master, teaching us the proper relationship to our tenuous grasp on life. There remained in the land of the living those who could never answer the question "why?"

There was, there is, and there will always be the land of Uz, the person Job, and the sons of God. And we shall also be there, fragile receptacles of a destiny we do not understand, partakers of a broken creation where we are called upon to know what cannot be revealed to us. Chances are most of us will remain comfortably within the masses of religious people in whom the sons of God take no interest. To be the instrument of a special divine vocation may bring to our days on earth sufferings and sorrows beyond our powers to endure. The Book of Job reminds us of how easily we belittle what we label "God's calling."

Perhaps we should welcome the comfort of anonymity and be satisfied with the performance of religious rituals which demand no specific response to the evils of the world and the suffering those evils inflict upon the innocent and righteous. Because there was a man in the land of Uz whose name was Job, the others were spared his kind of suffering. The wager required only one man, "the greatest of all the people in the east." The sons of God do not wage war against religious mediocrity, which already contains the seeds of its own destruction. The conflict must be well focused. God not only agrees with Satan on that point, but he also suggests a choice: "Have you considered my servant Job, that there is none like him on

. . . .

earth, a blameless and upright man, who fears God and turns away from evil?" There was only one savior nailed to the cross. The redemptive purpose of God finds its way to us through one representative at a time. The rest of the people are called upon to participate vicariously and through faith in the offer of redemption.

There was a man in the land of Uz who was for a time the focal point of a conflict which changed our perspective on God's creation and redemption. Once set apart by God, Job could no longer belong to his former world. Like Christ, he may have felt that he was in the world but not of the world, that human affairs did not fit any more in a scheme of things which appeared the more strange the more he tried to grasp and explain it. As in the case of Job, our destiny may be connected with some heavenly wager not known to us. Since we do not have the will, the patience, or the strength of Job, divine compassion may be expressed toward us by protecting us from a fate which would bring neither well-being nor redemption. But in times of suffering, justified or not, God places in our path the example of Job to let us know that he is never absent from our world, however absurd and unjust that world may appear.

. . . .

MEDITATION 2.

That man was blameless and upright, one who feared God, and turned away from evil. (Job 1:1)

n the land of Uz, Job stood on the fringes of events which were destined to transform not only his life but also the world surrounding him. He relentlessly sought a spiritual home he believed possible to achieve through meticulous religious performance and unimpeachable obedience to his God. Yet terrifying obstacles taught him that what is dearest to us may be taken away in order to fulfill a necessity God alone defines.

At the door of a ghost continent from which all of his cherished possessions were withdrawn, Job was overwhelmed by the intuition that in order to remain a loyal subject of God, he may have to suffer the loss of personal goods, security, and even logical reasoning. From the beginning of his new pilgrimage, he had to convince himself that the fear of the Lord cannot be made dependent on anything he would have liked to assign to it.

Job captured the attention of the sons of God, not because they had anything in common, but because he was blameless and upright. Through his striving for perfection, he could realize what the sons of God were incapable of, namely, turning away from evil. But the very evil he was able to shun through a conscious act of the mind and will was destined to alter his life for the worse, and this with the consent of God. Job had to rethink the fate of the righteous one. For a moment, his determination and moral strength surpassed the playful

. . . .

attitude of heavenly powers that show no mercy for human frailty.

Our vulnerability engenders a sense of indignation. We become the victims of evil while God chooses not to eradicate it. We search in vain for the proper scales on which rewards and punishments can be measured and meted out with justice, if not with compassion. Unjust suffering has always baffled those who cannot accept a fate that contradicts their notion of God. To rise above our traditional creeds requires a profound transformation in our religious commitments. The scholastic philosopher Duns Scotus, who spent a great deal of his efforts proving the existence of God, acknowledged the limitations of his own faith: "I believe, Lord, what your great prophet has said, but if it be possible, make me understand it."

The Roman philosopher Seneca was once asked what kind of comfort one could offer to those suffering unjust misery. He replied, "It is for man to take everything that comes as if he had asked for it, nay, as if he had prayed for it." When we proclaim to be ready for what God wills, how do we know that we can make ourselves will what God wills? Long before Seneca, Job had learned through hardship that the loyal friend of God is never without true comfort, and that God's presence is always consoling. But to us the presence of God may appear as either comfort or discomfort. Job knew both, and the wonder of his spiritual strength is that he stayed constant. Even in misfortune, evil can be refused a ruling place in life.

"There was a man in the land of Uz, whose name was Job; and that man was blameless and upright, one who feared God and turned away from evil." Spiritual and physical geography acquires a special meaning through those who appear within it with a specific mission. The land of Uz may have remained forever absent from human consciousness without the presence of Job.

Our determination to live in righteousness extends a redeeming dimension to the environment where our lives evolve. Place and person become inseparably linked. Saint Francis is no longer only Saint Francis, but Saint Francis of Assisi. There was a Moses transforming desolate places in the wilderness into sacred sanctuaries. Among the scattered tribes of Israel Deborah brought unity out of disarray. In the land of the Persians, Esther secured the deliverance of her people. John on Patmos, in the midst of desolation, gave human suffering a divine perspective through which time extended into eternity, and life into immortality. On the streets of India and beyond, Mother Teresa elevated human agony into cells of hope. Many more could be listed. With them as our spiritual mentors, we participate in the joys and sorrows of divine purpose.

In spite of the blessings that great people of faith can bring to us, the modern world can also claim the dubious distinction of transforming specific places into symbols of suffering. Names like Auschwitz, Treblinka, Buchenwald, Hiroshima, and many others are indelibly connected with a tragic sense of savagery. Some inscrutable destiny mixed with cruelty dislodged them from their peaceful place in history to evoke the dark side of human barbarity. They have altered our conception of places of importance on the maps of the world.

We contemplate with awe the Jobs of all times and their resolute devoutness in the midst of their tragic encounters with the cruelties of life. Sainthood arises from turmoil amid destructive forces opposing God's purpose. There was a man in the land of Uz, and we can now turn to him in our search for the meaning of suffering.

. . . .

When the sons of God entered the battle for the possession of the heart of Job, he had to make sure that he was in full control of his being, that he remained the repository of the moral and spiritual treasures he had accumulated through his faithful worship of God. To resist God's permissive behavior transcends our spiritual strength. Yet, Job is presented here as the model of faith unshaken by any of the rational conclusions of his friends. To know God is to know him in all ways of life and not only according to our expectations and norms. Whatever the specific obstacles placed on our way, Job will remain for us the model for such an achievement.

MEDITATION 3.

Questionable Success (Job 1:2–5)

ot all is well in the land of Uz. The enjoyment of life brings with it the fear of divine retribution. How does one make sure that God is not offended in the multiple situations which do not involve a consciousness of his presence? Job does not live with the risk of divine displeasure, neither for him nor for his family. After each feast given by his sons, he performs the necessary sacrifices to appease God in case of misconduct by his family. The roles are well defined. We must surrender to holiness, and God must forgive expiated sins. It is God who unifies Job's family. Thus, it is Job's responsibility to make sure that no sin persists within his household.

"Thus Job did continually." His name means, according to one derivation, "the penitent," the one in need of atoning for his sins and the sins of others. But his name also suggests enmity and hostility, strife with God, and a constant questioning of whatever is or might be. Job does not project the image of a totally satisfied life. Rather we find him continuously in a state of apprehension and anxiety. But it is an anxiety he tries to free from despair and an apprehension full of faith. This is what God's adversary fails to perceive as he underestimates Job's resilience.

The pervasiveness of sin does not allow us to gauge the exact impact it has on life, and ignorance of it can be as disastrous as a consciousness of it. Thus, Job chooses to offer sacrifices for the sins he knows as well as for those he suspects his family may have perpetrated without being aware of them.

As a conscientious *pater familias*, Job performs the rites of purification for his family. Little does he surmise, however, that the religious functions he hopes will save his household from divine disfavor will be of no avail in his own case. Through his agony, he discovered that the practice of prescribed rituals, however necessary they may appear, are not the only standards by which God evaluates human conduct. Were that the case, criminals and evildoers may find a boon in the exercise of routine rituals without any real wish to atone for their misdeeds.

The suggestion of Pythagoras, that human beings are at their best when they approach the gods, may find a serious challenge in the Book of Job. In some instances, the practice of religion remains self-serving. Through it we attempt to secure benefits for our temporal life and often fail to praise God for no other reason than his eternal majesty. Our performance of religious rites does not systematically put us in a safe category when evil is unleashed. On the contrary, the drama intensifies because of the righteousness of Job.

Every now and then, even at the peak of Job's happiness, a cloud comes to darken his good fortune, a suspicion that through the deeds of members of his family God's anger might alter the well-being of his household. He believes that he can atone for the sins of his family. No doubt Job seems peculiar to his loved ones and friends even before his misfortunes reveal his search for God in a way that surprises and sometimes angers them.

Job dutifully played his role of family priest, not surmising that future generations would find in his torments the gifts of holiness capable of being extended vicariously to those who seek redemption from their undeserved affliction. He believed that we can atone for the sins of others, as others can atone for our sins. Are we not constantly in need of friends who can atone for the deeds we fail to perform, for the kindness we fail to show, for the words of comfort we do not extend to others, for the compassion we are unable to muster at the very moment it is the most needed, and for the forgiveness we refuse to grant to those who offend us?

"Thus Job did continually." Routine and repetition could empty religious performance of its meaning. But not in the case of Job, for his responsibility was not to himself, but also to those he loved. The bonds which united him to the rest of his family could not be allowed to be shattered by sins, conscious or not. When others acted irresponsibly, he took it upon himself to secure God's forgiveness. Like Moses in the wilderness, Job would plead with God not to carry out his threats of punishment against those who were not capable of discerning his holy will, and like Moses, Job viewed his own salvation in the context of the fate of the people for whom he felt responsible.

No one could probe into the silent springs of Job's spiritual life or hear the voice of God speak in secret to his predestined role as an example for many. Did it make a difference that he felt so strongly for the happiness and wholeness of others? In a tumultuous world, he shared in the misfortunes of those God placed on his path. It was in the hours of Job's spiritual desolation that God made his voice audible to him, no longer in peaceful routines of religion, but in the whirlwind. In his torments, he no longer performed the rites of purification for his family. His wife counseled him to curse God in the name of justice and fair play. His children may have done the same, had they still been alive. True worship does not depend on whether we understand God. We must contemplate God in his eternal glory and majesty—even as difficult as that may be.

There would be no end to the inner transformation God operated in the life of Job. When success turned to failure, when sweetness changed to bitterness, when doubt replaced faith, and when hope was dashed by despair, the bonds that united Job to others also crumbled. The journey became solitary, and out of that solitude we could hear the supplications and prayers of Job no longer affecting his family alone, but piercing through a world in the constant quest to transform human chaos into order.

MEDITATION 4.

"Whence have you come?" (Job 1:7)

ow many places are there in the land of Uz where wanderers can hide from God's presence? Divine time and space leave room for the sons of God, and Satan in particular, to exclude themselves from the creator's vigilant eye while wandering among mortals in search of their prey. What does one learn from going to and fro on earth? And how does one discover divine intentions amid perceptions and perspectives often difficult to sort out?

A tour of our planet is quite revealing. Sometimes you do find the unexpected, a righteous and upright person. The sons of God were, in many ways, more successful than Diogenes, who even with his lantern in the daytime never found his honest man. Had Diogenes found his honest man, he would have glorified his virtues. The sons of God find in virtue and honesty a target for destruction.

The open land of Uz cannot claim full divine protection. No borders can keep Satan out and no limits are imposed on the number of ways people choose to live. In all the journeys of Satan, as well as in God's solicitude, one person is noticed: Job. One in so many thousands and millions. Where are the others? Why is Job singled out? Are there really none like him? Does he possess all virtue and all righteousness? Does humankind have to be reduced to one specimen to discover what it is all about? Job in his sores, Christ on his cross. Spiritual transfiguration leads to rejection and anguished solitude.

. . . .

"Whence have you come?" Does God expect a description or a travel log from Satan? Is freedom of movement so precious and so important that even God does not refrain from granting it to his own adversary? Or has God somehow admitted to having lost control of his creation, hoping that within it he may still find someone faithful and loyal while the rest of it goes its own way? We might entertain the idea that God respects our places of hiding. He can understand that we were not meant to live permanently and intensely in his overwhelming and majestic presence. We are naturally drawn away from him until our hearts grow sufficiently restless to seek peace within the realm of the spiritual.

The qualities of Job represent coveted elements Satan can no longer possess. They must be tested to ensure they are not endowed with preferential treatment by the creator. The governing of the world cannot rest on favoritism. If Job is righteous because he is God's favorite, he does not deserve praise. To make sure, anything that resembles divine privilege must be withdrawn, and Job must reveal his true nature. What would life look like at the moment when everything is taken away from us?

God's question to Satan ("Whence have you come?") resulted in a new necessity laid upon Job, a righteous person so noticeable in a world deprived of sacredness and holy devotion. Because of Satan's roaming Job was marked for a destiny which compelled him to wage war against the enormous arsenal of evil until, exhausted by the battle, he found himself in an impoverished circle of friends and foes whose hearts were no longer touched by the magic of wonder.

In the presence of Satan the attractive universe of Job dissolved into a maze of baffling and incomprehensible

. . . .

connections, his human mind now subjected to the annihilating power of doubt and indignation. Did God allow himself for a moment to play dice with the universe in order to vindicate a wager? Perhaps the proper question is, "Whence have you come, Job? You have reached the last shore of your earthly blessings, and the maker of the universe to whom you owe your life has now decreed that you shall live in desolation, though not in defeat, for nothing will ever exclude you from the divine circle of compassion which could never be complete without your presence within it."

Displaced from the center of his family life, from the successes he achieved through years of careful and loyal worship, Job must also fear to be abandoned by God and to have to find within himself the power to resist the intentions of the Evil one. He does not yet know that he will have to map out a new spiritual peregrination through psychological territories whose difficulties will be equal only to Satan's imagination. His universe will become a place of unexpected events. How long will he be able to live on the fringes of an open-ended, unpredictable spiritual world dominated by the wanderings of Satan rather than by the wisdom of his friends or the comforting presence of his God?

Do we expect to hear the same question when we approach God: "Whence have you come?" The modern world provides many hiding places from God. We have developed such a mastery of the worship of self rather than the worship of God that we often fail to know the difference between the two.

As long as Satan will be searching for his victims, the question will remain relevant: "Whence have you come?" For when we approach God and seek to live according to

. . . .

his purpose, he knows and we know whence we have come: from the restlessness of the world, from the tribulation of human events, from the feeling of discouragement, from the lack of faith, from the failure to hear the message, from the twilight of moral and spiritual exhaustion. And then, contrary to Satan, when we hear the question from God addressed to us personally, we may detect in it his fatherly compassion and his offer of redemption.

. . . .

MEDITATION 5.

"Have you considered my servant Job?" (Job 1:8)

hy ask? Surely God knows the answer to that question. Could Satan's roster of potential victims be hidden from God? Perhaps Job was high on Satan's list. In fact, he made it to the very top with no difficulty. Job's religious intuition led him to insights marked by a deep sense of scrutiny and questioning. There he was not safe at all. Indifference would have provided a stronger shield against moral and spiritual testing.

Strange indeed that Job's superior moral and religious qualities should be the reason for his temporary affliction. It might prove less troublesome for us to be lost in a crowd where most people concern themselves only with questions that have no importance for either God or the devil. To rise above this leaves anyone in the vulnerable position of a more defined target. That was Job's problem. He had become too conspicuous in his search for a righteous life. What came naturally to Job became a bone of contention for Satan. Could anyone do good for the sake of goodness? Is there a virtue which claims no other foundation but itself?

Here we confront again an insoluble paradox: divine blessings can unsettle their recipients. Job is transformed by Satan into a calculating person whose qualities are predicated on divine favor, not on personal merit. This is easy dialogue indeed between Satan and God—no contest on either side as far as the major rules are concerned!

. . . .

Often we are willing to serve God in return for special blessings, especially temporal success and eventual redemption. After all, rewards and punishments have always been the guides to the land of the religious. Curiously, Job was different, but not obviously so.

"Have you considered my servant Job?" Is it possible that the challenge might be too great for Satan, that Job could frustrate his sense of confidence? There was something in the desperate nature of the world that gave Satan the advantage, that exposed the weakness of human expectations in an elusive divine purpose. Job might just be able to reverse that through some unusual fortitude, converting moments of anxiety into occasions for spiritual renewal. The sons of God could not have foreseen that, in the case of Job, peace would be the result of dissatisfaction, of discouragement, and of communion with a suffering God. No one ever knew the true source of Job's unshakable trust in God, certainly not the sons of God who failed to make him helpless in the midst of incredible agony.

We never know whether the principles on which we base our lives are valid until they are tested. Should life depend on the presence of good or bad fortune? Or should it have its own essence, unaffected by the precarious expressions of everyday life? Lady Philosophy rebuked Boethius because the turmoil which beset him had overshadowed his true nature. To know oneself in the perspective of the good while living in the midst of evil is what Boethius and Job had in common, one in the name of reason, the other one in the name of divine righteousness.

The land of Uz has now become the residence of one special person, a witness to divine wisdom on whom the

. . . .

mysterious heavenly rays will converge and then reflect again to enlighten a world in distress. The rest matters very little. The cosmic forces will concentrate at one point. The conflict will be relentless, the outcome of utmost importance. Sir Francis Bacon asserted, "By the agency of man a new aspect of things, a new universe, comes into view." Do the human mind and will have the power to defeat what is and replace it by a new order?

Job was not destined to change the world, just to show that God's presence within it can be troublesome and intriguing when it comes to our notions of security and comfort. He has been selected for a strange test no longer involving only his person. It is a test of the very essence of a world torn apart by the conflict between the forces of good and the forces of evil. He may have been in his own time the only person God could present to Satan for the vindication of all that still exudes universal goodness in his creation.

. . . .

MEDITATION 6.

"Does Job fear God for nought?" (Job 1:9)

ince the functioning of creation relies on divine providence, it is natural that religion has been made dependent on God's blessings. The gifts bestowed by God on his people should serve as a proof of divine satisfaction, as the recompense for loyalty and obedience. Strangely enough, this proof of divine satisfaction does not work convincingly in the Old Testament. God is made to question the value of his blessings. Yahweh often laments through the prophets: "I have done all those things for my people. . . . Yet they have forsaken me."

In fact the question of Satan ("Does Job fear God for nought?") is quite appropriate. What is the real source of religion? Would it collapse if privileges were withdrawn? Or is there also a moral and spiritual foundation to our understanding of the divinity, a foundation which possesses its own validity independent of visible forms of divine favors?

The expectation of rewards diminishes the authenticity of worship. Satan thrives on such a proposition and offers his challenge: "Does Job fear God for nought?" Does anybody ever fear God for nought?

Paradoxically, Satan was about to take religion out of the context of vulgarity where God is cast in the role of a beggar for the loyalty of his subjects. Thus, our behavior determines the moods God finds himself in—angry when we misbehave, happy when we praise him. Even Satan knows the vulnerability of such a perspective, and he is about to test it.

. . . .

The correlation between Job's possessions and his worship of God becomes the center of Satan's argument. If human beings could be seduced to remain within anthropomorphic perceptions of God, then the forces of evil would win the battle against transcendence. God would have meaning only within the context of our earthly pilgrimage. To a great extent, routine daily life does not concern itself with transcendence for the very reason that it does not develop a strong sense of the sacred. The realm of redemption is often reduced to advantages we derive from it and is thus emptied of awe and fascination.

Would we still worship God for the sole reason that he is God, that we owe him our reverence as the creator of the universe, even if we received nothing in return, not even salvation?

In an age of enlightenment and rational reasoning, we have grown accustomed to setting our own terms for our relationship to God as if he had to comply with our spiritual, moral, and ethical norms. We naturally search for a religion with which we feel comfortable. Thus, even our adoration of the Lord is sometimes determined more by our notion of rights and privileges than by a sense of humility and compassion, as if God owed us a spiritual life conforming to our wishes and beliefs.

Satan's question ("Does Job fear God for nought?") now belongs to the universal voice of all believers, for a true worship of God can only be for nought. The only thing we can bring to God when we stand in his majestic presence is ourselves freed from pretense, illusion, and self-importance. When we end up believing we understand God and his word, we are guilty of spiritual arrogance, for a God we could comprehend would cease to be God. We so often distort the ultimate purpose of religion by putting so much of our self-importance into it that, as

. . . .

Durkheim suggests, we slide into self-idolatry by worshiping ourselves while believing we offer our reverence to God.

There is, however, a level on which the question of Satan becomes irrelevant for those who contemplate divine majesty in love and trust. There is a communion with God which takes us beyond the search for personal comfort and security, to a willingness to let our being be dissolved into God's being. There is a sacredness which we discover when, in our own secret places or in our houses of worship, we enter into the presence of God with fear and trembling.

Job's quest frightens us, for it does not allow for a consistent view of religion, for a well-defined relationship with God. From rebellion to trust, from anger to equanimity, from despair to faith, he crosses the infinite spaces of all possible human responses without ever losing sight of the need to remain within God's compassion. The important questions are no longer whether Job understands God or why he fears and worships him. Job seeks to persuade himself that his torments and misery will not annihilate the bonds that have kept him close to his Lord for so long.

Perhaps we are destined to find God when he no longer makes sense to us, when he transcends all of what we can say, think, or believe about him. But Satan knows the liability of the human condition, and he persists in expecting the failure of Job. He has roamed earth long enough to feel confident that, in the absence of specific favors, God will fail to be worshiped on a large scale.

And what about divine jealousy? Can even the sons of God endure to look at the way God showed special

. . . .

consideration to Job at the expense of others? Do we sometimes approach God with the Pharisaic notion that we are entitled to more blessings than other people? Was God fair in allowing Job to have enjoyed so many advantages in what appeared to be a spirit of favoritism while neglecting those less inclined to serve him with the same zeal? Absolute justice should rest on absolute equality, but absolute equality would reduce God to simple neutrality. Religion thrives on inequality, on a principle of contradiction, on a dialectical set of impossible connections. Job does not yet know what makes him righteous. He simply assumes a stance which makes him blameless and upright.

Satan does not know, or wishes to ignore, that the wonder of grace can move human hearts as much as material gains, and, in Job's case, more so. But the sons of God also know that few people wish to experience the ideal that Job strives for or to share the wisdom he silently proclaims. The marriage of heaven and earth is visible only to the very few. For the multitudes it is couched in riddles beyond their concern. Satan has simply chosen the wrong victim.

Does Job worship God for nought? Can religion survive in the absence of divine favors? No answer can yet be provided for Satan's astute question. The wager must run its course before Job becomes the visible evidence of a loyal subject of God who no longer anchors his spiritual and moral being in his earthly possessions or, for that matter, in his traditional religious expectations. Were the prophets right in pointing out that the performance of ritual religion may in fact be a hindrance to the discovery of mercy and justice? Why did Jesus reject a great deal of ceremonial and Pharisaic approaches

. . . .

to religion in favor of a search for the fundamental goodness of the redeemed heart? Did Job already know, ahead of his time, that the springs of spiritual life do not reveal themselves until we lose a great deal of what passes for religion?

. . . .

MEDITATION 7.

So Satan went forth from the presence of the Lord. (Job 1:12)

aving won the first part of the wager, Satan finds himself in a position of unexpected freedom, a kind of declaration of independence which gives him the liberty to act according to his own decisions and impulses. To obtain such independence, one must depart from God and no longer feel the constraints of moral and spiritual responsibility.

The Marriage of Heaven and Hell cannot subsist for long. Soon the whole cosmos loses its spiritual harmony in what may be described as *The Divorce of Heaven and Hell*. God and Satan part company, leaving bewildered sons and daughters of man amid worlds in collision, seeking for what can no longer be found and surmising what can no longer be clear. In all instances there are now two ways: The way of heaven and the way of earth. While Job yearns for God, he must suffer the devastation inflicted on him by Satan.

Job refuses to compromise. The way of the Lord is hidden behind the stratagems of God's adversary. The freedom of Satan brings oppression to the righteous one. The small and great dramas of time no longer find their expected resolution. Bodily pain may reduce our physical world to nothingness, a card Satan will play to its bitter end. But what he ignores is that the soul of Job is no longer in contention. What could a victory over the material goods mean if Job refuses Satan access into his spiritual being?

. . . .

In his unexpected plight Job does not understand why he is subject to Satan's torments, nor does he know how he might circumvent happenings which bring only terror. God has hidden from Job the meaning of his quagmire, so seemingly relentless and destructive. He cannot yet surmise that through his calamities, multitudes of sufferers in generations to come will find a way to peace and redemption. Often we must abandon or modify what we once had or believed and accept drastic changes affecting our temporal perspectives and our view of eternity. Satan departed from God's presence. Where are the limits to the evils he can unleash on the world? Is there a curse in freedom as much as a blessing?

How strange that a certain form of freedom requires a disconnection from God, a positing of our own wills, the feeling that we are responsible only to ourselves independently of a universal law which tries to find its way to our minds and hearts. Satan no longer cares for the totality of anything. He simply wishes to accomplish his desires. Is that not the way to true and undeniable achievement?

To depart from the presence of God means disconnecting ourselves from the source of existence and being. We act as if we are no longer in need of awesome relationships. Wrapped in our cocoons we end up finding the rationales for our self-sufficiency. Self-righteousness springs from ignorance and our limited view of reality. We are more efficient in our small corners. There we do not owe anybody anything. Satan is satisfied with the knowledge that he can exercise his right to deal with Job as he wishes. Even God now withdraws some of the limitations he first put on Satan.

The wider world of Job is unknown to Satan. We seldom recognize that our mistakes in life come from the

. . . .

fact that we have severed our ties with the larger realm of the living and the dead. The wisdom Odysseus searched for, he found when he visited those who preceded him to the underworld. There Odysseus learned that if we want to proceed judiciously in life, our knowledge must include the wisdom the dead left as a legacy. Wisdom belongs to the vast reservoir of the human experience from which nothing can be deleted without affecting our universal being.

Freedom and independence must be qualified. They mean very little in themselves. They acquire their power from accumulated perspectives and trials of generation after generation. Satan chooses not to know that.

Going forth from the presence of God! Is that possible? The whole universe is filled with his presence. Why then is there room for evil? Do our spiritual and mental states allow us to entertain the notion that perhaps, somewhere, God has withdrawn from the scene to let evil dominate in the lives of his children? Heraclitus reminds us that "To God all is perfect and excellent. But men must see all things as either good or evil." Evil increases in proportion that we remove ourselves from a search for the meaning of divine intention. Our divine vocation can never be understood apart from our participation in both the human and the divine. Again we find in Heraclitus a stirring suggestion when he urges us to consider that whatever is divine becomes progressively human, and whatever is human is ultimately experienced by God. Then he adds, "Immortals become mortals, mortals become immortals; they live in each other's death and die in each other's life."

. . . .

Job symbolizes our collective participation in what appears to us as either good or evil. His story spans the abyss allowing us to cross from one aspect of reality to the other, wondering at what point we may land on the shores of perfect understanding and serenity. A journey with Job is a journey into the collective purpose of creation, however concealed it may be from our present gaze. The common bond of humanity overrides our selfishness when we realize that we must remain intimately related to what constitutes our collective destiny in a divine creation. This is where Job will prove greater than Satan.

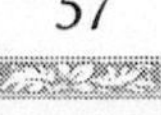

MEDITATION 8.

"Naked I came from my mother's womb, and naked shall I return." (*Job* 1:21)

he whole of life is played out between birth and death. We start without privilege and end without advantage. Does that make life absurd? From nothingness to nothingness. What benefit can either God or Satan derive from dealing with what has meaning only within such a limited span of time? Job's material possessions were destined to give only temporary satisfaction, for they could not cross over to the eternal. Was Satan taking away from Job what Job would have lost anyway?

Fair play was not a part of Satan's plan. It never is. In the case of Job one also wonders about God's fairness. Some divine requests may seem heartless, as when God directed Abraham to sacrifice his son as a test of his faith. Finally the act did not take place and God was praised for his compassion. But Job was not asked for anything, a more baffling predicament. He could not even prepare himself for the loss of his children, nor could he consent to it in faith or object to it through rational discourse. With God's acquiescence, Satan ensured that Job would not become a willing participant in the drama. Job did not even raise the question: "Where is God in all of this?" Faith escapes definition.

From a human point of view, vanity rules supreme. Christ warned us against our propensity to amass treasures on earth. They do not belong to the stuff of eternity. But what about life itself? Are the sons and daughters of Job nothing but pawns in the hands of either God or Satan, the prize for strange wagers over which Job has no control? Whatever else we may come to possess, life never belongs to us in its totality. Job knew that life is entrusted to us only for a short time by a God who never relinquishes control over it.

"Naked I came from my mother's womb, and naked shall I return." Having lost everything, Job fell upon the ground and worshiped God. In the presence of his creator, he let his mind wander from the womb to the tomb. From the womb he emerged from darkness into light. Now he knew that at the moment of his birth he was translated from God's eternity into the struggle of existence.

In every birth, divine purpose loses its purity until at death we return to the darkness of the earth. In our pilgrimage through the uncertainties of life, we let ourselves be encumbered by superfluous possessions and desires until we lose consciousness of our divine destiny. Instead of responding to his calamities with anger, Job worshiped God. Even in tragedy he could distinguish between the essential and the superfluous.

When Michelangelo was questioned on the creative power that allowed him to sculpt his David, he replied that the gift of the artist consists in seeing the statue in the marble and in proceeding to remove the superfluous. In reality, he said, he did not carve the statue. Rather he sought to discover its essence, an essence that was always there underneath. We, too, must learn how to remove the superfluous—that which does not belong to our lives, that which creates our limitations. Too often we are condemned to carry within us the accumulation of superfluous material that weighs us down and prevents us from coming to the awareness of our true humanity. We cannot create beauty, nor do we produce masterpieces in the strict sense of the term. They are contained in our souls and intellects. The question is rather: will our hands and our thoughts obey the divine purpose, as we liberate the beautiful and the good from the limitations that veil our true identities?

But how could Job worship God in the loss of his children, the most precious possessions of all? They were God's gift, and certainly not in the realm of the superfluous. Yet it was God's intention to let Job feel the power of his own being which possesses nothing but itself. Can anyone contemplate life from such a perspective?

The tragedy of the world does not come from the absence of goodness but from our inability to deal with the superfluous within which the beautiful and the good are lost. In our temporal situations the superfluous becomes the important, and tragedy and catastrophe are much too often the result of ignorance. A great deal of what keeps us down to earth is congenial neither to the soul nor to the intellect. Lost in the mazes of passions and emotions, in our assurance of self-righteousness and in our sense of duty to the immediate, we fail to sense the permanent and the perfect. Goodness exists without our participation in it. But it seldom discloses itself to us because it cannot get through the layers of the irrelevant.

Redemption consists essentially in removing what does not belong to life, in escaping self-imposed burdens of materiality, in rediscovering our inner beings as they were intended by the creator. Could it be possible to reduce everything to a rudimentary simplicity and admit that as long as we deal with the superfluous we remain unable to see the essential? Who can save us from such a process? We seem destined to live amid the greatness of God's creation, though unwittingly ensuring that it will remain hidden from us as we drift from tragedy to tragedy, farther and farther away from God's purpose.

. . . .

What then is our ultimate responsibility toward life? The question is neither raised nor answered by Job. It suffices for him to know that he is chosen by God as a receptacle for God's gifts. The God who gives and the God who takes away remains the God to be blessed. "In all of this Job did not sin or charge God with wrong" (Job 1:22). It takes great effort not to apply to God our standards of justice and fairness. When life's events sharpen our sense of indignation, Job reminds us that sin may consist in judging God's actions according to our expectations.

Job is the opposite of Satan, ready to acknowledge his full dependence on his Lord. The gift of life is not to be argued or possessed. It is to be experienced while we have it with the expectation that it will be returned to us transformed, redeemed, and eternal. When Job heard of the misfortunes of his family, he rent his clothes, fell to the ground, and worshiped. His sense of loss was never disconnected from his duty to acknowledge the higher power of life. Certainly there was injustice in all of this, but life was not to be surrendered to mere rationality but to faith, and faith implies the mysterious.

MEDITATION 9.

"You moved me against him, to destroy him without cause." (Job 2:3)

ivine hesitation? Divine reproach? Did Satan make God do something he did not want to do? Have we misunderstood creation and God's relationship to it? Can God really protect what Satan marks for destruction?

The wager about Job's life seems to reveal Yahweh's instability and the momentary power the adversary is allowed to enjoy. Creation does not yet rest firmly on its foundation. God's masterwork still exhibits too many flaws. Leviathan threatens to throw it back into chaos at any moment. The intrusion into the human world of the sons of God severely distorts the original purpose of creation.

The situation becomes even more complex and discouraging when the writer of the Book of Job depicts the sons of God as more vigilant, more astute and sometimes more aggressive than God himself. Creation suffers from a divine complicity which remains beyond logical analysis. Jung saw in it the major cause of human tragedy: "The inner instability of Yahweh is the prime cause not only of the creation of the world, but also of the pleromatic drama for which mankind serves as a tragic chorus."

How could the presence of Job influence any of that? If, as Jung points out, "Even God seeks his goal," then it may be that God needs Job. God needs the best of his creation to bring the struggle to a redemptive end. God needs the body of his faithful. He needs the minds and the hearts of those who can see that beyond all the inconsistencies of temporal life, we can reach redemption and

. . . .

fulfillment. We shall never fully comprehend why the world is as it is. But we must assume our place in it with all our strength, determination, and faith.

The fortitude of Job resides in his ability to proceed beyond his questioning of God's action into a moral and spiritual stance that defies Satan's stratagem. In the midst of torment unjustly inflicted on him, and even when frustration seems to destroy him, the word "failure" never becomes part of his vocabulary. He may have sensed what Blake expressed when he wrote, "All that can be annihilated must be annihilated," an insight repeated by Goethe's Mephisto: "Everything created is worth being liquidated." Has not God relinquished too much of his dominion to allow Satan to achieve his end? God himself presented the bait to Satan: "Have you noticed my servant Job?" How could Satan not seize the opportunity?

As the best in God's creation, Job was called upon to deny what appeared as ineluctable finality. Through his religious intuition he discovered divine images unassailable by logic and reason. How much of the Book of Job can we still understand while applying to it our rational categories? Job simply did not entertain the concept of inconsistencies. He could rise above them and never cease to worship God.

The freedom of Satan must be challenged by our own freedom. This is difficult when we feel alone and abandoned in our decisions. There are no clear means to overcome the obstacles placed on our way, nor to know whether they are the will of God or the doing of Satan. We may be annoyed by God's wearisome forbearance of Satan in the case of Job. We may also ask the very pertinent question: "Why doesn't an omnipotent God pull evil up by the roots?"

. . . .

The absurdities of the world often dictate our own absurdities. It is often in the most tragic moments that the will of God is the least discernible to us. Our sense of urgency may mislead us into believing that God's solicitude should accompany us in special ways, mostly when the world collapses around us. I recall the anguish we experienced as a family in France during the Nazi invasion in World War II. War had come very close to us, and fear ruled our lives. In desperation we packed a few belongings and joined in the vast exodus of people trying to flee the devastations of war. Little did we know that we were moving in the wrong direction and that we would fall in the hands of enemy armies three weeks before they reached our empty homes. We never found an answer to that kind of "why." Disorder within God's creation seems to operate according to its own principles, often invisible to our minds and hearts.

Job had to concede the fragility of the created order. Nothing within it is secure, and righteousness does not guarantee divine favor. Quite the contrary! The closer we come to God, the more we experience the turmoil of a creation yearning for its fulfillment. Job found himself not in a perfect world, but in one that does not yet fully belong to a sole creator.

When Paul suggests that this world has been handed over to its rulers, does he echo what Job had to discover at such a heavy price? It shocks our religious sensitivity to read that God was moved by Satan to the point of allowing the destruction of God's own. Certainly no one would dare to be literal at this point. There must be a hidden meaning behind such a proposition—well hidden indeed! Or are we the victims of the imagination of the story teller in the Book of Job, a poet whose sense of

. . . .

universality led him to reduce all powers to the same level of purpose, whether on the side of good or evil?

The fact that God allowed himself to be influenced by Satan has troubled believers of all generations and is not likely to receive a satisfactory explanation within our ways of thinking. It was only after Job lost all his possessions, including his loved ones, that he understood that everything depends on God. What he had been proclaiming through his religious dogmas and practices struck him now with the force of a new revelation. If God is truly impenetrable, mysterious, and inscrutable, then it is impossible for us to understand and judge his actions. Consequently, it does not belong to us to comprehend, and much less to explain God's attitude toward Satan.

God's mysterious behavior takes us on a path of faith which leads beyond the case of Job. Divine providence may not be visible in the world of daily routines. For those who can decipher the message, the Book of Job provides an insight into imperfection and terror, into evil and injustice, as well as into the eternal dominion of God.

Having given the green light to Satan, does God withdraw from his creation? Will it be Job's responsibility to place God back where he belongs? Will he be able to generate within himself the faith that will compel God to vindicate the ways of righteousness against the objections of the adversary?

It is strange that Job is portrayed in the story as the only one who does not vacillate, who shows more consistency than either God or Satan. In a way, he has become the Archimedean point from which the rest of the spiritual

. . . .

universe is moved. For a moment, according to this text Satan has the power to persuade God. Until the roles are changed again, the center is occupied by Job whose aplomb and stability are meant to influence even divine decisions. Job defies all religious logic by remaining faithful to a God who acknowledges that he has allowed his destruction without cause. Is Job already embodying humanity in the role of the suffering servant?

. . . .

MEDITATION 10.

"Curse God, and die." (Job 2:9)

isorder within God's creation brings disorder within human life. Where does one turn for justice when it no longer exists in the divine realm? God assumes that Job can retain his integrity even in the worst of afflictions. But for that to work, God has to make sure that Job's righteousness remains unshaken when he discovers that divine blessings can also generate high levels of suffering.

Rationality does not belong within God's equation. The wife of Job voices the purest form of logic. Integrity must receive its reward if it is to be pursued further. If Job is cursed by God without reason, it becomes his right to curse God with good reason. What is it that Job knows, but his wife fails to perceive? Is it fair on the part of Job to reproach her for being a foolish woman? Is she not suggesting a fair application of Moses' principle of the *lex talionis*? There was no doubt about the universal appeal of such a principle which had originated with God himself. In fact, Satan claims credit for it, as if he had been the originator of such a law of conduct. He challenges God to let him use his own principle of "skin for skin."

It may have been daring for Job's wife to apply to God his own law: Eye for eye, tooth for tooth, curse for curse. But she also knows that one does not contend with God and that the end of it will be death. Even so, she cannot exonerate God from obligation to a law which he commanded Moses and all his people to obey.

. . . .

Because of Job's moral strength, his family was able to create a small world of their own within God's world. Everything pointed to divine blessing reinforced by a sense of fairness in the game of life. There was no logical way to understand why Job was stricken so suddenly and so completely. The wife of Job was determined to demand the reparation of a wrong she believed God had done to them. In her conviction to be right, she dared lodge the wrong directly onto God and tried to convince her husband to agree with her.

Suffering as well as happiness may accompany us in our search for truth. But it is usually impossible to sustain a steady equanimity throughout the process. Job's truth is no longer shared by his wife. Both partake of the same intensity of awareness, but it pulls them apart as they view the process and the end of it from different points of view. Job continues his journey of unshakable belief in God's providence; his wife adopts the stance of all or nothing. Finding herself in the situation of nothing, she requires the vindication of her concept of justice. Interestingly enough, she does not curse God herself. Such a responsibility belongs to the *pater familias*, the priestly father who is left with no option but to acknowledge God's injustice.

The equation of life for Job's wife is plain and logical. God has no right to withdraw moral and spiritual security. She is not prepared to confront an empty world. She is not willing to subscribe to the wisdom of many sages who have tried to find equanimity by accepting a reality that cannot be altered in its ultimate end. Lucretius expresses the dilemma in plain terms: "The substance of this vast world is condemned to death and ruin." To that Epictetus adds: "We spend our time in waiting and we are all condemned to die." Yet we cling to the world and do not want to abandon it.

The turmoil inflicted on Job and his family shattered the links that have united Job to his wife for so long. We do not know how it all ended nor what kind of transformation took place in the life of Job's wife. But we know that Job did not curse God. His quest for truth eluded those around him. What price is one willing to pay for the discovery of truth? Dostoevski has Ivan Karamazov proclaim, "If the suffering of children serves to complete the sum of suffering necessary for the acquisition of truth, I affirm from now onward that truth is not worth such a price." What kind of a God would require the death of Job's children to teach him a lesson in truth?

Philosophers as well as victims of unfair cruelties have often regarded the nonexistence of justice as the most serious threat to ethical conduct and as the greatest obstacle to religious persuasion. But to consider God unjust is what Job refuses to allow himself and those around him. The real question is not whether God is just or unjust. We do not possess the standards by which to measure those assertions. Rather, we should question why our norms of justice clash so definitely with whatever governance the world is endowed with.

Some Church Fathers were not willing to grant Job's wife any wisdom. Chrysostom suggested that every time she spoke, the devil was at work in her, for the advice she gave was never consonant with what he thought to be God's eternal will. In the same fashion, Augustine considered her as the instrument of the devil. But he also used the instance to demonstrate the strength of Job in opposition to the weakness of Adam, who, according to Augustine, also lived in the company of a foolish woman.

. . . .

Whereas Eve had been able to seduce Adam, the wife of Job is unsuccessful in altering her husband's stand.

Job's wife assumes that human righteousness is directly connected with divine perfection. When such a bond is broken, indignation receives its justification. When Job's wife cries out, "Curse God and die!" her anguish seems warranted, for she feels that rebellion and death are preferable to unjust suffering. For those who greatly suffer from injustice, should not death be welcomed as the last vindication? How wrong was Job's wife?

MEDITATION 11.

"Shall we receive good at the hand of God, and shall we not receive evil?" (Job 2:10)

ob's universe remains holistic, though subjected to contradictory forces and principles. Divine wisdom which brought the world into existence will also lead it to its final purpose. Good and evil mingle as two sides of creation not understandable within the physical order of the cosmos. We should accept whatever the hand of God dispenses. The receptacle does not choose what it must contain. Job understands this and thus avoids the intolerable frustration of dealing with a God who seems to disregard the sanctity of life.

Job progressively retreats within the ill-defined zones of faith where submission to the will of God precludes debate on propriety or justice. The pressure to apply to God human values was mounting, and Job had to deal with the fragility of religious commitments, mostly when those commitments conflicted with rules of ethical conduct.

There comes a point where submission to divine will dulls the acuity of reason and intelligence. Job did not sin, we are told, by accepting his fate without trying to alter it in spite of the advice of his friends and family. Righteousness is not argumentative or vindictive. If the self must be dissolved into the divine essence, it has first to learn how to accept all aspects of that essence as it expresses itself in both positive and negative ways.

Job wondered why no one can be a true recipient of God's blessings unless and until one had also been tested

. . . .

by the negative forces which emanate from God. He was not willing to concede that God's majesty could express itself as what appears to be a curse. In the presence of evil, we are not victims of tragic flaws but courageous bearers of a fate we confront with moral and spiritual strength. We are the symbols of a destiny against which nothing can prevail. Can Job prove greater than all of this?

Job's wife has slowly established the norms and rules by which life is to be measured. In this case, God does not pass the test. His providence turned into undeserved tribulation directed at one of his most loyal subjects. For a moment at least, Job tries to view his condition as being in harmony with divine will. He does not yet realize that he has become an important actor in a drama, and that without him the play could not proceed to its resolution. Against his will he has become an important piece of the puzzle without knowing what the entire picture looks like.

Our yearning for God owes its source to the fact that we cannot forever be faced with a decision between good and evil. At one point or another, the struggle must lead to peace and equanimity. True, if there were no evil we could not appreciate God's providence and protection. No one can penetrate the divine wisdom that God used to create a world he could not free from terrible conditions. No Gnostic speculation can provide an acceptable answer. Freedom in such a world comes as a small consolation to those who regard it as a fatal gift dooming them to defeat. The divine purpose opens up to our understanding when we discover that in creation God suffers too, and that suffering creates our common redemptive bond.

. . . .

With Job tragedy resides in a suffering caused by good, not by evil. Had Job been a perverse or immoral being, his fate would appear normal. But he has learned how to be tolerant of evil as the creator had to be tolerant of it. This, however, does not constitute any excuse not to struggle against it as God himself seeks to eliminate it.

William Blake remarks, "the roaring of the lions, the howling of wolves, the raging of the stormy sea, and the destructive sword, are portions of eternity too great for the eye of man." The outcome of our mental striving is not harmony and peace, but apprehension and uncertainty. If all manifestations of life are part of eternity, then we do not understand eternity, for we have been accustomed to make a distinction between good and evil, between that which creates in us a yearning for eternity and that which hopelessly and tragically keeps us bound to our earthly predicaments.

Wisdom invites us to contemplate our destinies as they have existed forever in the universal mind without blaming the divinity for what we cannot comprehend. It may seem strange that the destructive side of nature could be turned against life without affecting eternity, which contains all evils without distinguishing them from the good. Could eternity be real while the cosmos is in such turmoil?

"Shall we receive good at the hand of God, and shall we not receive evil?" What does the human eye and the human heart perceive within the limitations of our temporal prisons? The reality of suffering should convince us that it will remain a part of the present, but that it will not cross into eternity. The evil we receive now, with the permission of God in a restless universe, cannot serve as the norm and standard of the final divine purpose. For as

. . . .

long as our earthly pilgrimage will last, we shall continue to experience life in its dual aspect of good and evil. Happy is he who knows that God is in control of both, and that the sufferings of the present age can purify our souls and make them acceptable for life in the endless eons of the new creation.

. . . .

MEDITATION 12.

The Day that Should Not Have Been (Job 3)

fter the first contact with his friends, which lasted for seven days and seven nights without a single word exchanged among them, Job broke the silence to curse the day of his birth:

"Let the day perish wherein I was born,
 and the night which said,
 'A man-child is conceived.'
Let that day be darkness!
 May God above not seek it,
 nor light shine upon it. . . .
Why did I not die at birth,
 come forth from the womb and expire? . . .
For then I should have lain down and been quiet;
 I should have slept; then I should have been at rest."

Job 3 belongs to one of the most poignant poems of the Bible, maybe of all literature. In it we find a parallel of Jeremiah 20:

Cursed be the day on which I was born!
The day when my mother bore me, let it not be blessed!
Cursed be the man who brought the news to my father,
"A son is born to you," making him very glad.
Let that man be like the cities which the LORD overthrew without pity;
let him hear a cry in the morning and an alarm at noon,
because he did not kill me in the womb;
 so my mother would have been my grave, and her womb for ever great.
Why did I come forth from the womb to see toil and sorrow,
 and spend my days in shame?

. . . .

Seldom do we hear to this degree the passionate plea of those who feel deprived of peace and rest in a world they do not understand and that does not welcome them. Job resented the harassment of friends and family in a situation from which God had seemingly withdrawn. Jeremiah voices his complaint against Yahweh, whom he accuses of deliberate deception. It was not in a moment of ecstasy, but as the result of a lucid analytical reflection on his existential situation that Jeremiah exclaims, "Cursed be the day on which I was born," and this in the same breath as his statement of indignation against God: "O LORD, thou hast deceived me, and I was deceived; thou art stronger than I, and thou hast prevailed. I have become a laughingstock all the day; every one mocks me." Jeremiah knew that the prophetic words he was speaking could no longer convey the depth of his encounter with the divine. He would have preferred eternal silence.

According to Ecclesiastes, "the dead who are already dead are more fortunate than the living who are still alive; but better than both is he who has not yet been, and has not seen the evil deeds that are done under the sun." Theognis, a Greek poet contemporary of Jeremiah, says that "for man the best thing is never to be born," a wish Einstein echoed as he wrote to his sister with a sense of discouragement at the thought that he was unable to help his parents: "Really it would have been better if I had never been born. Sometimes the only thought that sustains me and is my only refuge from despair is that I have always done everything I could within my small power."

Like Job, Jeremiah, Aristotle, and many others, Theognis and Einstein would have preferred the state of

. . . .

nonbeing. To assume conscious life is to meet the antagonistic forces which conspire to eliminate us from a world that was not meant to become our permanent abode. So, why enter it at all?

Blind and tormented Oedipus sat on his rock at Colonus, still fearful of a destiny that has surrounded him with tragedies. Depleted mentally, morally, and spiritually and trudging through the desolation of physical exhaustion that only his two faithful daughters can alleviate, he hears the distant chorus sing what was supposed to be his consolation: "Nothing surpasses not being born; but if born, to return where we came from is next best, the sooner the better."

Even those who have been privileged to penetrate a great deal of the mysteries of the natural world have been overwhelmed by the feeling that our participation in creation must remain an awesome puzzle. Teilhard de Chardin who more than most scientists has viewed the physical world through the eyes of faith writes: "It is a terrifying thing to have been born: I mean to find oneself, without having willed it, swept irrevocably along a torrent of fearful energy which seems as though it wished to destroy everything it carries with it."

Every birth adds to the accumulated absurdity of life, and every death promises a return to eternal serenity. But death is no longer welcomed by those who have tasted life. Thus, many Greeks and Hebrews would have wished to avoid the choice and subscribed to the the idea that the best thing would be never to have been born.

Both Jeremiah and Job arose against divinely ordered destinies which remained indifferent to their individual plights. There is no reasonable explanation for the fact that those who are supposed to mirror the greatness of God must do so at the price of great suffering. Indignation and revolt turn to the nostalgia of eternal nothingness which can no longer exist after we become conscious of time. Why fight the leviathans of the world that even God could not overcome? Did God expect mortals to achieve what he himself could not?

Do Jeremiah and Job know something that escapes us? Can their curse come from a knowledge we may never attain? Having been chosen by God to see more clearly the troubles besetting a broken world, how could they avoid wishing they had never become a part of it? But time always proceeds forward, and that which is can never be undone. Cursing the day of one's birth, even with all the power of poetic imagination, can never erase that day from either divine or human memory.

We carry the burden we did not choose, for who would choose to be born with a knowledge of what life will mete out to its participants? What can we learn from that which constantly rejects us? At some point in life we may wish to make the prayer of the Psalmist our own: "LORD, let me know my end, and what is the measure of my days; let me know how fleeting my life is!" If we were meant for eternity, why should we have to experience the limits of time?

Both Job and Jeremiah imply that when life surges in front of us in all of its terrifying aspects, who would choose to be born? Thus, we come to formulate for ourselves a certain yearning for nonbeing. The price we pay for the possession of the mind and for the ability to know both good and evil often contradicts the promise of a fulfilled life, hence the belief that eternal nothingness would solve both the despair of being and the yearning for nonbeing.

. . . .

The double scales we weigh everything on are not always properly adjusted. No one in a normal course of life wishes the day of death more than the day of birth. Why then even suggest such a choice? Is life as we experience it just an interlude in God's peaceful eternity? Do we not feel sometimes, as Job did, that what preceded our earthly existence and what will follow it is preferable to the turmoil of our human days? Everything that mingles with time and mortality is deprived of its essential goodness and meaning. The dream of eternal innocence is interrupted by the act of being, and the consciousness of evil prevents the resumption of that dream. Wisdom alone can redeem us from despair and annihilation. But, like Job, we must keep the faith that what precedes time and what constitutes eternity cannot be destroyed by the events of temporal life.

Yes, birth is the most natural of all events and, according to the writer of Psalm 139, a wonderful act of divine creation. Yet Job has to appeal to the forces of nature to come to his help as he tries to justify his negative feelings toward what should have been a successful life. Perhaps blessing consists in not being known by God. There is better security in the anonymity of crowds, and Job may have preferred to stay there among the wise, the crafty, and the successful. With God he has no rest and no peace. His unhappiness comes from the fact that his misery is enlightened by a divine insight which reveals a world at odds with all traditional conceptions of it. His friends will try to comfort him, not knowing that, in fact, they will add to his suffering. His world is no longer the same as theirs. The curse itself must die, and life must go on until it reaches its eternal quality free of despair and anxiety.

MEDITATION 13.

"Is not your fear of God your confidence, and the integrity of your ways your hope?" (Job 4:6)

ogether with Bildad and Zophar, Eliphaz sat silent in the presence of Job for seven days and seven nights. When wisdom retreats, words become useless. God created the world in six days. Eliphaz tried to rebuild it in seven. The pieces of the puzzle refused to fall into place. God's creation was afflicted by flaws beyond explanation. It belonged to Eliphaz to reconnect divine wisdom and human events. He assumed a realm of justice which guarantees the rewards of righteous living. The misfortune of Job must be attributed to his own failings, however hidden and perplexing, and not to unjust and undeserved divine chastisement.

To Eliphaz, Job appeared as a fallen giant, incapable of mustering enough patience to consider his condition in realistic perspective. Even under the best circumstances, spiritual fortitude does not guarantee that we will find the strength to overcome our predicaments. In this world, no person can claim to be so perfectly happy and fulfilled that something at some point does not threaten his or her well-being. Human affairs keep us anxious and uncertain.

Eliphaz acknowledges the store of spiritual blessings Job has accumulated. But why can none of that lead to a resolution of his difficulties? Certainly Job can bear his misfortune with equanimity. But is it misfortune? Are we the judges of what we label good fortune or bad fortune?

. . . .

Eliphaz operates within the norms and conventions upon which all could agree. But there are cases where nothing is as miserable as we believe it to be. Job's insight into his plight has already led him to rebuke his well-meaning wife. He may now have to do the same with his friends, though they are the ones praising his exceptional spiritual qualities.

Happiness never remains long with those who claim to possess it. The greater the claim to happiness, the more painful it is when it abandons us. Once the greatest man in the land of Uz, Job is now regarded the most miserable. Not even his friends can grasp the situation.

Job, however, remains in control of his world. He may have already sensed the truth later expressed by Christ, that those who can kill the body have no power over the soul. You cannot force anything on a free mind, no matter the depth of physical suffering. Job is determined to show that even in his torment, he can find peace in a world of chaos. Where else but in such a world does one need spiritual strength?

Certainly the plight of Job must be of short duration. Even Eliphaz knows that Job's confidence cannot be shaken and that his integrity cannot be questioned. Patience and time will resolve it all. Indeed, it will, but not according to human expectation. Job had to learn that in some cases traditional religion fails to reassure us. Perhaps it is not meant to.

Job is capable of more self-analysis than Eliphaz gives him credit for. As a true friend, Eliphaz is dismayed by what has happened to Job. But he is also concerned with what could happen to his own world, should God continue to violate the principles of reciprocity whereby righteous conduct ensures divine approbation. There is a principle of verification at work in religion as well, and Eliphaz will utilize it as a vindication of God's action. But, for the time being, the equation does not work, for what is happening to Job is normally reserved for those who commit iniquity.

Since the flaw cannot be in God, it must be in Job. How simple! It should suffice now that Job find again his confidence through the fear of God, and his hope through his integrity. He must undertake the journey back into his former life in order to try to discover the cause of his failure. Neither Eliphaz nor Job could ever surmise that they have been isolated within the cosmic drama to play a role which they did not define for themselves. At that point the traditional values of religious life no longer apply. If they did, Satan would have an easy victory.

. . . .

MEDITATION 14.

"Think now, who that was innocent ever perished? Or where were the upright cut off?" (Job 4:7)

trange question indeed! Where have you been, Eliphaz? Your religion is full of presuppositions, but seriously lacking in facts. You challenge Job to think about innocence. Have you thought about it yourself? Innocence does not exist, cannot exist. It belongs to a divine experiment which lasted a very short time in a nostalgic past no one can recover. It was possible only within the dream of the garden, and not even all of the garden.

Innocence requires a very small cosmos, manageable within the limited resources we can bring to it. In the wider world east of Eden, where everybody lives under the curse of the knowledge of good and evil, it would take divine wisdom to know the difference between the two. God's adversary knew then, as he still knew in the days of Job, that confusion comes with knowledge and that the dream of innocence could survive only in an archetypal memory that accentuates suffering rather than well-being.

Evil does prosper on earth! In Gospel wisdom, Christ made the divine element in us dependent on our understanding of the Father's providence toward all, making his sun rise on the evil and the good, and sending rain on the just and the unjust. Spinoza reminds his readers that good and evil fortune is distributed indifferently among the just and the wicked. Socrates' statement that no good can come to the wicked and no evil to the good does not verify itself in our daily predicaments.

. . . .

When nineteenth-century Romantic writers speak of a universal sadness, they refer to the perplexing fact that evil can be deeply rooted in a world guided by a good helmsman. That evil not only exists, but goes unpunished and leads to a sense of universal injustice. The plights foisted on so many innocent people seem to belie the omnipotence of God. It seems a God of love and mercy would deprive the evildoer of the power to achieve ends contrary to our welfare. But both divine providence and human fate refuse to fit neatly into our categories of thinking. There is a fundamental disequilibrium in creation that escapes our understanding and sometimes even eludes divine redemption. The sophisticated debates between Job and his friends could last indefinitely without acceptable results.

Forgetting one's true nature can become the source of inner struggle. Boethius' voice of wisdom reminded him that the cause of his misfortune was due to a lack of knowledge of himself in a world of conflicts. What appeared to him as the triumph of evil came from fundamental ignorance. "It is because you don't know the end and purpose of things," says Lady Philosophy, "that you think the wicked and criminal have power and happiness. And because you have forgotten the means by which the world is governed you believe these ups and downs of fortune happen haphazardly."

The religion of Eliphaz presupposes a world where good and evil are precisely delineated. But if such a world exists, the very notions of guilt and innocence could no longer apply. For in a world of absolute excellence, everything would be flawless and in no need of correction. What Eliphaz does not remember is that, because of our loss of innocence, we have invested our ingenuity in creating mythological dreams in order to ensure our salvation.

The innocent who do not perish never belonged to a human world. One becomes human only through the loss of innocence and through the courage of accepting death for it. The world of Eliphaz has no reality and certainly could not bring comfort to Job. There are no models Job could emulate, and the sophistry of Eliphaz could only reinforce a negative view of reality, that iniquity automatically brings retribution.

To our dismay, we are led to acknowledge that injustice has been more profitable than justice. Religious leaders and philosophers of all times have labored without success to uncover the reasons why the quest for justice remains an endeavor fraught with pervasive danger. For that reason, pretense to justice, rather than justice itself, has ruled the world of human affairs. Listen to Plato's character Glaucon: "The just man will have to endure the lash, the rack, chains, the branding iron in his eyes, and finally, after all extremity of suffering, will be crucified, and so will learn the lesson that not to be but to seem just is what we ought to desire." This argument of Glaucon was sternly refuted by Socrates.

How would one apply the notion of innocence and justice to the world of Job or the world of Christ? Why did God allow the massacre of so many small innocent lives, not yet two years old, simply because Christ appeared on earth? Should we blame such an act on the coming of Christ or on the evil nature of Herod?

There would be no nobility in a world perfectly well organized around precise and definite principles. Such a world does not stir anything within the soul because it does not correspond to anything we experience. But the

. . . .

undeserved suffering of the just in the struggle against evil has often been the source of inspiration for those who wander through the perils of existence.

Yet Eliphaz is right at one point. Rational life cannot rest on haphazard and chance events. It must be governed by some principle of justice or face continuous chaos. Rulers of all generations have ensured the punishment of the wicked. But some have also destroyed innocent lives in the name of dubious claims.

Sainthood and martyrdom would not exist in a world that could establish perfect norms of rewards and punishments. It is the uncertainty and vulnerability of our decisions that require divine wisdom, far beyond the little of it most of us can secure. To know oneself in close communion with God only makes us more aware of the fragility of all events. To be willing to pay the price for the flaws of creation exceeds the spiritual capacity of most of us.

Innocent people have perished, and the upright have been cut down. Under the rule of absolute justice, where the innocent are rewarded and the evil punished, Job would have never been known to us. It is because the usual rules of ethics and morality no longer apply to him that his whole being is transformed into a battleground upon which new perspectives will develop. The innocent are destroyed and the upright are cut off because they are subjected to standards and norms that do not correspond to their affirmation of life.

For all his good intentions, Eliphaz cannot penetrate Job's world, because that world does not fit into the rational structures of justice and holiness. Even within the religious world, justice is practiced less for the sake of justice itself, than for the reputation people can derive from it.

. . . .

Though honorable, the practice of justice is much too laborious, and few are humble enough not to let their left hand not know what the right one is doing. Innocence could be achieved only in a world free from evils, in which case it would no longer deserve praise. In the absence of innocence the only way open to us is to accept our mortality and our fallibility. To deny them would make our world unreal.

How are innocence and justice to be viewed in a world from which God has chosen to withdraw temporarily? Can there be anything more oppressive than God's silence? Job has just started a long and solitary journey with no expectation of divine support. His friends unsuccessfully tried to put the proper perspective on his numerous frustrations and fears. God has not touched them, which appears to be a blessing. But it will also prevent them from knowing the depth of Job's experience.

If innocence and righteousness are to exist again, they must be born anew from the depth of anguish. To find in God's creation what for a long time has ceased to be obvious is indeed the discovery of the divine within us.

MEDITATION 15.

"Can mortal man be righteous before God? Can a man be pure before his Maker?" (Job 4:17)

ransitoriness and mortality preclude any ultimate knowledge of righteousness. God does not expect us to discover the norms by which righteousness can be defined and implemented. Were it so, we could overcome the power and reality of death, a proposition God would not allow. Thus, "mortal man" cannot be righteous before God, though he may come to know what righteousness entails.

So, there we are trying to explain what should be left alone. We are not the creators, but the victims of the flaws of creation. There is no solution to Job's plight because there is no solution to the created order. Judeo-Christian religion knows that and has carefully crafted a way out of a theological impasse by proposing the idea of a new creation. There divine and human norms will meet in some fashion that will preserve both a memory of the past and a regenerated life.

Job does not have the support of a new creation. He must accept the only one he knows and not rebel against it. Realism can find a place even within religion when one dares consider the divine acquiescence of evil. How else could redemption be understood, but as a moral necessity on the part of God to account for the destructive forces against which mortals have no protection? Divine compassion rests, at least partially, on the premise of a God who feels a deep obligation to salvage his investment in a humanity from which he has been spiritually severed but without which he would lose his status of creator.

. . . .

The deeper we penetrate the mysteries of creation, the more our mortal nature surges into our consciousness. Our yearning for unity with God is frustrated by what separates us from him. Teilhard de Chardin expresses such a feeling in a moving prayer: "All of us, Lord, from the moment we are born feel within us this disturbing mixture of remoteness and nearness; and in our heritage of sorrow and hope, passed down to us through the ages, there is no yearning more desolate than that which makes us weep with vexation and desire as we stand in the midst of the Presence which hovers about us nameless and impalpable and is indwelling in all things."

The fifteenth-century German philosopher and prelate Nicholas of Cusa viewed our limitations as "learned ignorance" in opposition to God's infinity. He spoke of God as being far away, in fact so far away that it would be better for us not to try to reach him. In humility we should accept our mortal destiny which precludes perfection. It has been an axiom of many thinkers that no moral law can change human nature, much less solve individual moral problems. Says the Russian philosopher and theologian Berdyaev, "The chief difficulty of moral conflicts is not the choice between obvious good and obvious evil, but the absence of any single, morally binding solution laid down once for all and the necessity for making each time an individual creating act."

The mystery remains. Why hasn't God resolved to eliminate what is contrary to his nature and replace it with a perfect act of creation? But every act of creation contains within it part of the essence of the creator. Thus, destroying his own creation, even in its imperfect state, would mean for God the annihilation of part of himself. Since this is not possible, he has to accept imperfection for as long as necessary and admit error even among his angels, as Eliphaz points out.

So, Job is much more than a victim. He becomes a test case, a divine experimentation in human resilience. Job will determine the limits within which God's relationship to his creation remains possible. The question is not whether we can be righteous and pure, but how close to divine essence we can be brought in the slow process of redemption.

MEDITATION 16.

"Man is born to trouble." (Job 5:7)

liphaz must travel a perilous path as he makes himself the defender of God's ways while recognizing the tenuous situations anyone can be thrown into. The leviathan at God's gate is also the one claiming his due in our heart and soul. In a troubled and threatened creation, we must share the tragic role of actors whose script lacks a conclusion. In an unfinished universe, everything remains contingent on incomplete propositions. Before the world was made there was no darkness, for there was no physical reality to contain it. Now our physical beings are hopelessly blended with the finitude of a world that conveys to us its instability, its threatening forces, and its promise of death.

Man is born to trouble, but certainly not by sheer divine design! Of the great works of creation, why are we so mean a part as to be tossed by fortune amid earth's wretchedness? If, per chance, God has not yet assigned a fixed destiny for the world, how could we hope to find one for ourselves, one that would give us security and assurance? Could it be that we are born to trouble because that is the only way we can partake of divine essence?

The idea that God suffers with us may not be acceptable if we consider the divinity free from what affects us. Yet many have found comfort in the knowledge that suffering keeps us close to God and strengthens our communion

. . . .

with him. Meister Eckhart says, "If God is with me when I suffer, what else shall I want. . . . God, suffering with man, suffers incomparably more in his own way than man suffers for him. It is therefore quite fair that I should suffer if God is willing to, for it is only right that I should be willing for all that God wills. I pray all day as God directs: Thy will be done. And yet when God wants suffering I complain, and that is wrong."

The Old Testament has always been concerned about the fate of the righteous, and throughout the biblical message we learn that suffering brings us closer to God. That being the case, suffering is the point of convergence for both God and his children. Certainly we could attribute suffering to God without being anthropomorphic. But there is more to suffering than what emerges from human experience. Job's turmoil is not only personal. The whole of humanity participates in it.

During a recent illness, my physical strength, so long taken for granted, diminished to the point that I felt powerless and frustrated. Pain and suffering forced me to view life from a different perspective. I became intensely aware of my new world, leading me to a sense of loneliness. It was then that I realized what I had often surmised, that in suffering we are never alone, that there are thousands of people who feel what we feel, who pray the way we pray, who seek comfort even when little of it is available. I became conscious of the existence of a suffering community. I understood more than ever before the redemptive aspect of pain. There is a tacit force in the world, often invisible to those who do not suffer, and sometimes even to those who suffer, a force rooted in divine compassion and human anguish. The sufferers of

. . . .

this world are not the rejected children of God, but the chosen ones capable of witnessing to God's presence through their prayers, their faith, and their hope. The suffering community often ignores its power and relevance in a world progressing from chaos to redemption. In my quest to know better this fellowship of suffering in the world, I came upon a text by Teilhard de Chardin in his *Hymn of the Universe*. I would like to quote it in its entirety because it expresses my thoughts and feelings very closely:

> Human suffering, the sum total of suffering poured out at each moment over the whole earth, is like an immeasurable ocean. But what makes up this immensity? Is it blackness, emptiness, barren wastes? No, indeed: it is potential *energy.* Suffering holds hidden within it, in extreme intensity, the ascensional force of the world. The whole point is to set this force free by making it conscious of what it signifies and of what it is capable. For if all the sick people in the world were simultaneously to turn their suffering into a single shared longing for the speedy conclusion of the kingdom of God through the conquering and organizing of the earth, what a vast leap towards God the world would thereby make! If all those who suffer in the world were to unite their suffering so that the pain of the world should become one single grand act of consciousness, of sublimation, of unification, would not this be one of the most exalted forms in which the mysterious work of creation could be manifested to our eyes?

Eliphaz is correct. There is an inexorable destiny connected with every birth, and every human journey is marked by trouble. In vain will Job accuse God of having changed good fortune into calamity. When weighed on divine scales, human affairs are always fraught with anxiety.

. . . .

Paradoxically, our search for peace and tranquility often discloses God not as a supreme being unaffected by any developments in his creation, but as a God whose compassion compels him to know the limitations imposed on his own work. Suffering does not mean that God has forsaken his creation. On the contrary, it reveals to us a depth of being which extends into eternity. The mystery of existence can never be disconnected from that suffering.

The wounds of Job are certainly more than the results of a bet between God and Satan. The protection of Adam in the Garden of Eden or the blessings of Job while he was in his secure estate did not lead to the knowledge of a God whose creation is still yearning to be set free from its bondage to the forces of evil. To be born to trouble may well be the first step toward the discovery of our eternal destiny.

. . . .

MEDITATION 17.

"Happy is the man whom God reproves." (Job 5:17)

he Septuagint, a Greek translation of the Old Testament produced in the age of the Ptolemies, translates the saying as "Blessed [*makarios*] is the man." The same Greek word *makaria* is used to denote blessedness and foolishness, probably to emphasize how elusive the search for blessedness may be in a world of foolishness.

Many writers of antiquity, especially Aristotle and Philo, considered blessedness to be an attribute of God alone. To share divine qualities, we must participate in the forces involved in creation. Blessing cannot be equated with absence of turmoil. Rather it denotes our understanding of the world as it essentially is, namely as God's creation in all its aspects, even those that might seem antagonistic to life. To search for the meaning of divine intentions is also to discover the vulnerable side of our earthly existence. Thus, Eliphaz's word of wisdom to Job: "Do not despise the chastening of the Almighty."

How does one establish a proper connection between God's way and our way? Being so different from each other, such a connection must of necessity rest on contradictory propositions. How could anybody be happy when reproved? How could anybody be grateful for receiving punishment while expecting praise?

There is certainly more here than the paternalistic theory of a God who must punish those he loves for their own good. Such an interpretation is sorely insufficient.

. . . .

Rather the holy person must partake of the pangs God suffers while in the process of bringing his creation into fulfillment. The chaos that threatens human order also seeks to annihilate God's creative work.

God's rebuke is accompanied by blessedness. This is again a contradiction difficult to resolve, for it finds its solution not in a rational evaluation of life and justice, but in the faith that God's creation cannot forever be subjected to destructive forces. In the meantime, we live in a reality within which God dispenses blessings and chastisements as part of the same process. One enlightens the other.

Occasionally we find Job on the verge of blasphemy. He has reached the limit within which his praise of God is still possible. He recognizes that he is only human and entertains the possibility of divine cruelty. Several times he has wished for death, the ultimate end of both good and evil. If there is any mercy left, then God should push his reproach to the point of death.

The plea of Job, though unusual, does not surprise us. It reaches its climax in his complaint to his friends: "O that I might have my request, and that God would grant my desire; that it would please God to crush me, that he would let loose his hand and cut me off! This would be my consolation; I would even exult in pain unsparing; for I have not denied the words of the Holy One. What is my strength, that I should wait? And what is my end, that I should be patient?"

It is universally believed that when the wicked receive punishment, they receive something that is good. Chastisement brings improvement to their brutish nature. Without punishment they would become only worse and

. . . .

deserve still greater chastisement. But how does one come to know the source of adversity and whether God agrees with it or is the author of it? Would it not constitute the greatest of all injustices if God should blame an innocent victim? What kind of atonement could there be for sins one did not commit?

If everything which happens in creation becomes part of God's memory, then errors once committed subsist in all eternity. The hope of Job is that God may have mercy on the guilty, whatever the misbehavior. It was not in Job's hands to decide what kind of fortune he would fashion for himself. Nor can he comprehend his misfortune and the intensity of divine anger.

"Happy is the man whom God reproves." Perhaps. Only through punishment can the wicked attain to some degree of goodness. But from the beginning, Job was touted by God as the most righteous person who could turn away from evil. Divine retribution does not seem appropriate, nor would it improve Job's standing in front of his creator. Why then does he wish for death?

Job will finally know God in suffering, and God will come to know Job in the same way. Having been linked together by the same qualities and attributes, they will also belong together for eternity. How else could redemption have meaning, if not as a deep common identity between God and Job, between God and all of us, an identity which does not allow blessing apart from suffering until the day when God himself will have put an end to that suffering?

. . . .

MEDITATION 18.

"Teach me, and I will be silent." (Job 6:24)

ven in the best of contexts and with the best of intentions, arguments among friends reveal the inadequacy of speech. Inner turmoil is mirrored in words that fail to convey the depth of thought. Silence may be preferable to the attempt of translating into language what was meant to remain a secret part of oneself, mysterious and inscrutable even to friends. "How forceful are honest words!" Certainly, but also how few. The standards by which God measures honesty are inaccessible to our perceptions. Thus, "let your words be few," advises wisdom. The fewer, the more powerful!

Through the wisdom of friends, we may find the clue to our calamities, if our silence could prevail long enough for us to hear not only their words, but also their intentions and feelings. Silence does not engender passivity. If that were the case, we could not learn anything from it. Rather it creates in us a receptive disposition toward calm and equanimity. Through silence we can weigh the sincerity and meaning of friendly suggestions and know whether they can move our hearts to be at peace or to remain in conflict.

The frailty and shortcomings of human words threaten friendship at the very moment when friendship is the most needed. The more tragic the situation, the fewer the right words at our disposal to meet the challenge. God alone is able to translate to Moses his everlasting essence in one word: *Yahweh* (I am). To mortals, that same God could

. . . .

reveal his purpose for them in ten words (the Decalogue). Eternity inscribed in so few words! But when errors enter the arena of human interrelationships, words multiply until they become so oppressive that only the yearning for silence provides hope for a soul in search of peace.

"Teach me!" Was Job willing to open his heart and mind to those from whom he could expect but little help? Could the inferior serve as a guide to the superior? Or does friendship allow degrees of meaning? The sincerity of one human being may conflict with the sincerity of another. But should that put an end to friendship or force us to live in perpetual suspicion? Is it not the case that we often learn from unexpected sources, sometimes even within the deliberate errors of those who claim to be our friends?

Job's friends think that they can teach him why and how he erred, though they have no insight into his plight, which originated in heaven and must play itself out on earth. The curse of ignorance persists and accompanies most of us to our graves. Virtue resides in the acknowledgement of our limits. How often has destruction been meted out to the human race by those who claimed absolute knowledge!

"I will be silent!" Words of wisdom? Words of resignation? Words of despair?

Does the world of Job allow for silence, or does it compel innocent victims in a drama even God cannot fully control to raise their voices in indignation, in fear, and sometimes in self-righteousness? When God chooses to remain silent, we are left with only human words. A desperate situation becomes even worse. Redemption comes when God's silence is met by our silence, by the

. . . .

power to still in us the voices of doubt, anxiety, and despair.

Exasperated by the trappings of a religion which no longer points the way to God, Kierkegaard exclaimed: "Disease has overtaken the world and the whole of life. If I were a doctor and I were asked for my advice, I should simply say: Create silence! Bring men to silence! The word of God cannot be heard in the noisy world of human affairs. . . . Therefore create silence!"

Strange indeed. It took the friends of Job seven days and seven nights before they could utter any word of consolation to a friend whose suffering was beyond expression. During that time, their deeds were more powerful than any speech they could have uttered. When they saw Job for the first time, all they could offer was their tears. They tore their clothes and sprinkled dust upon their heads, imploring heaven to take notice of their common contrition. They sat with Job on the ground for a whole week.

Silent compassion? Words might destroy the magnanimity of their vicarious participation in the suffering of a friend. Judgment will come on the friends of Job as soon as they resort to speech, for in speaking we reveal prejudice and pettiness, even with the best of intentions.

Shortly after my arrival in the United States, I was called on to minister to a family who had just experienced the loss of a loved one. Still ignorant of some of the customs of my new environment and still lacking fluency in my new language, I felt totally inadequate for the task. How could I bring solace to the bereaved? What could I say? How would I say it? As in the case of Job's friends during the first week with their stricken companion, I sat silent with those in need of consolation rather than offer

. . . .

words or eloquent speeches. After I left, I realized the family had done most of the talking and I felt I had failed. For weeks thereafter, the family kept thanking me with fervor for all the help I had provided. I was surprised, and I learned a valuable lesson. It is difficult for us to understand that the genuineness and intensity of our spiritual presence can communicate our communion of heart and mind, more than anything we can say. In their suffering, the bereaved can hear words which are never spoken. Spiritual communion transcends our ability to verbalize it. Not that words are unimportant. They still represent the best means to convey our thoughts. But through the divine gifts which endow our beings with worth and permanence, we can always be more than what we say or intend to convey.

It is surprising to realize how little the disciples remembered of what Jesus said and how often they disagreed on the meaning of it. They were frequently puzzled by the silence of Jesus. Sometimes they wondered more about his silence than about his words. The disciples knew that in front of the glorified Christ, words lost their meaning. Faith provided the foundation for their new relationship. It placed the disciples, and all of, us in constant expectancy, discovering again and again that we shall never comprehend God's mystery in its totality. When the Lord is in his temple, the earth should remain silent.

When tragedy crosses the boundaries of the bearable, words cease to translate the reassurance which comes from God alone. To offer ourselves as a presence in times of sorrow may require our words of comfort. But like Job's friends we may begin with a recognition of our inadequacy and with a deep sense of frustration at our inability to communicate to others what we sincerely believe to be God's message to them.

. . . .

When all else fails we may contemplate the mysterious and the inscrutable through the eyes of wonder and faith and find peace by realizing with Thomas Merton "night is our diocese, and silence our ministry."

Elijah found God in a whisper, Jesus met him in the solitude of the mountain, Job in the depths of despair, Viktor Frankl within the confines of barbed wire, and Mother Teresa in the ravaged faces and bodies of the poor. All of us meet God every day, often without discerning his presence, in all the circumstances surrounding us, as we silently extend our acts of compassion to those unable to see the rays of divine love and providence.

Wonderful and powerful words accompany us on our journey through life. They come to us in their creative and redeeming force. God's Logos penetrates deep within creation and within our souls. But when God speaks we no longer hear words in their human form. Meaning comes from silence. Like Job, we may grope to know where we are in our temporal situation, deprived of peace and wholeness. At times we speak, and at other times we listen. When we learn how to listen to silence, we may hear the divine voice gently leading us to a vision of that which remains incomprehensible. We, too, may be destined to hear God proclaim silence.

. . . .

MEDITATION 19.

"I loathe my life; I would not live for ever." (Job 7:16)

espite the hardships of existence, hatred of life is not a common feeling. If it were, we would remain permanently discouraged and would not attempt to bring correctives to what we despise. Hardship may occasionally lead us to question God's intentions toward us. Life can indeed be unfair, if not absurd.

So far in the wager, Job has had as his daily bread only disruptions and frustrations. He has accepted his insignificance, but at the same time he can no longer restrain his indignation. His past successes now appear to him as fragile achievements that have fallen prey to the forces of disorder.

In an eloquent burst of emotion, he contends with an invisible God whose presence he would rather avoid. Anger has brought him closer to God than rational discourse: "I will speak in the anguish of my spirit; I will complain in the bitterness of my soul." And in all of this, he knew that there was something greater than what he felt and thought at the moment, something that would remain beyond his grasp.

Hatred of life results from the inability to find peace with oneself. In his torments, Job would have welcomed the rest of the night while on his bed, as he attempted to flee into the simplicity of sleep and away from the strains of self-consciousness. But that is exactly the moment God chooses to scare him with dreams and

. . . .

frighten him with visions. And what could be more debilitating than a continuous string of nightmares sent to mortals by the divinity?

God often chose to disclose his will in dreams and visions. Sleep provided an escape from the limits of time and space. Dreams can create worlds of their own, and God can use those worlds to make his purpose manifest to those who cannot discern him within logical thought. The torments of Job become even worse in his dreams. His mind can no longer impose rational reasoning on frightening events. While asleep his life is totally under divine control, and he finds no comfort in such a situation. The fear of the night evokes in him the abyss of divine anger.

Is not Job entitled to some compassion? God appears to him as a hideous creature from whom he can no longer escape. As a result, he proclaims his hatred of life and his wish not to live forever. What indeed would be the meaning of eternity if it were plagued by the flaws inherent in this life? The thought of eternity as a mere continuation of time becomes unbearable within the realistic context of Job's experiences. If God can dispense so much misery in so short a time, who would wish to remain in the hands of such a God for all eternity?

When life is disconnected from its divine source, and when, as in the case of Job, God drives a wedge into the fabric of our being, separating us from him, then the feeling of revolt is born out of a deep sense of absurdity. As long as Job must wrestle with his own temporality, it seems to him more compassionate on the part of God not to grant him eternity. Thrown back upon himself, Job assumes the courage of his own being. That

. . . .

courage excludes perpetuity which would only formalize endless suffering.

In an unexpected twist of events, Job has to start a painful descent into chaos. Gone are the days of his success, days which may have prevented him from coming face to face with his destiny. Will he find God in chaos? Will he recognize his own true self there? We cannot seek order without a knowledge of chaos. The archetypal fight of God against the original chaos survives in all of us and compels us to search for our true self in the midst of what seems antagonistic to life. Job thought he had found the leverage point from which his world could be moved. His friends approached every situation with the same confidence. But in a world of tragedy, we find many Archimedean points as we view every situation with a new heart and a new mind.

Job can hardly bear the thought that God can violate the sanctity of life. Should he thus search for his own solution to his plight? Job does not want to hear the advice of his friends, for he knows that he alone can reflect on his situation, which seems empty of basic goodness. Why cling to life after it has been divested of joy and promise? Not only are the days of mortals on earth few, but they are marked by extreme hardship.

The worst that could happen would have been for Job to rationalize his situation. The cogent advice of his friends appears empty and irrelevant. He simply does not comprehend why God should pay that much attention to him, since the result is testing and torment.

For a moment, Job was drained of all resources and overpowered by a strong sense of unworthiness. He slid from well-being to misery, from happiness to tragedy, from a sense of inner peace to anxiety, from hope to despair. When nothing is left, the will to live also abandons him. According to Paul, Christ experienced some of what Job felt, as he left his divinity in heaven so he could, in his earthly form, share the anxiety and suffering of those he came to call to redemption.

Job is beginning to sense something greater than the need to explain everything. Maybe life is meant to be mysterious, and it is altogether possible that a logical approach to things might destroy our relationship to God rather than enhance it. Job's loathing of his life represents not only an act of rebellion but also a profound statement on humanity.

Fulfillment in life may not reside in what we can explain and understand, but in what we can create out of the remnants of our spiritual and moral endowments. Perhaps we should not live forever. The best way to oppose suffering and injustice is to assign to them the limits of time, and not allow them to cross into eternity. In a mysterious way, Job feels that extending his life *ad infinitum* would mean nothing else than giving misery an undue advantage. So his prayer to God is simply, "Let me alone." Not the most usual of prayers.

. . . .

MEDITATION 20.

"Why have I become a burden to thee?" (Job 7:20)

he joy of creation stops when the final product no longer corresponds to the ideal pattern from which it evolved. Creation as we experience it in the context of sin differs from creation as it was conceived in God's mind. Most prophets emphasized the chasm between God's ways and our ways. Yet, they never gave up on the basic bond which unites both.

Job finds himself at home neither with God nor within his own world. No longer does he reproach God for his misery. He becomes almost apologetic to God for being where he is, an object so far removed from the divine ideal that no reconciliation seems possible. The image of God in him has turned into an unrecognizable blurred picture.

But why should Job feel responsible for the flaws of a creation deprived of perfection and harmony? Is it not God who burdens Job rather than the contrary? Yet, it has been the mark of our humanity to feel guilty for situations beyond our control. We feel ill at ease within creation. Basic laws of equilibrium have been broken, and we search in vain for some original realm of innocence which could explain our transition to a fallen state.

We have become a disturbing presence in God's universe, not knowing where we belong or what our destiny entails. Thus, we have also become a disturbing presence to ourselves, as Martin Buber reminds us: "Man becomes a real problem to himself when as it were the original contract between the universe and man is dissolved and man finds himself a stranger and solitary in the world."

In his former state as a successful person who could share his material and spiritual wealth with his world, Job enjoyed a profound sense of self-fulfillment. He would not have even entertained the thought of being a burden to anybody, much less to God.

Now Job appears to us as a wanderer through the desolation of life and homesick for a lost world of tranquility. His life amidst a purposeless mosaic of broken fragments keeps him wishing for an elusive realm of unity. His failure becomes deeply personal. Yet he shows enough nobility to consider himself the source of his misfortune and feel guilty for being such a poor representative of God's creative power. He has come to symbolize the human yearning for a life at peace with itself and with God. Along the journey he is overcome by a sense of unworthiness, by the conviction that in his search for redemption, he can be nothing but a burden to God. For the time being, he must remain the wanderer, the *homo viator*, who has not yet discovered his destination.

The story of Job teaches us that when we are deprived of a knowledge of our true self, we may never come to know the nature of the universe that contains us. Our sense of loneliness comes mostly from the fact that we no longer grasp the connection between our temporally conditioned mind and the universal mind of God. Thus, what else can we be in the world but strangers? We do not belong to it long enough either to understand it or, even less, to transform it.

It is our destiny to wander amidst mysteries never to be grasped, seeing the obvious, yet never knowing it.

. . . .

Job's demise serves as a parable of our human condition. We shall forever argue about the meaning of life and wonder why God persists in attributing so much importance to it. In the process we shall continue to search in vain for security and permanence. But the test Job must endure is meant to reveal that even Satan cannot break the bond between creator and creation. Were that possible, both we and God would stop being a burden to each other. But we also would proceed to our instant death, away from our source of life.

Throughout this portion of Job's soul searching, he always assumes he is the transgressor, the one who violates the sacred bond of divine relationship. Yet, it is Yahweh who breaks all those bonds and plants in the heart of Job an exaggerated sense of transgression. How could God forgive something he is the author of? Is the writer of the book of Job allowing us to entertain, for a moment at least, the possibility of divine perversity? Why should Job, in his very innocence, become the victim of a contest between God and Satan? Does cosmic fair play exist?

Job assumes that he is automatically the guilty party. He knows that redemption requires that he not question God's ways, but submit in obedience and faith. Yet he cannot dismiss the thought that perhaps God plays a game with the world and that he does not know the rules of that game. In such a game, God always has the upper hand.

As the story of Job shows, we are not taken into the confidence of divine decisions. The uncertainty of the journey, however much it may be grounded in faith, is never free from doubt and anxiety. Job does not take God's forgiveness for granted. His challenge to God is that someday he will no longer be a burden to him. With

. . . .

death he will enter a realm where even God may no longer find him: "Why dost thou not pardon my transgression and take away my iniquity? For now I shall lie in the earth; thou wilt seek me, but I shall not be."

MEDITATION 21.

"Inquire, I pray you, of bygone ages." (Job 8:8)

ith Bildad we meet the second voice of rationality in the dialogue between Job and his friends. We are invited to assume that the universe reflects a perfect design that was more evident in previous ages. Consequently Job must scrutinize the past to find in it the verification of God's perfect relationship to creation.

Many Hebrew writers share with Greek thinkers of antiquity the idea of moral and spiritual decadence. Socrates believed that the ancients were better than his contemporaries, closer to God and to the truth. Thus, we meet a paradox: the more we progress in knowledge, the farther we remove ourselves from divine participation.

Most of us surmise that there is something hidden in the wisdom of the ages. Every generation has contributed to the accumulation of human knowledge, creating a tacit dimension of life not always apparent to us. Job complains to his friends that all have failed to discern the divine intelligence which ensures order in creation.

Our nostalgia to recover what was lost with the giants of the past aggravates our sense of failure. Bildad suggests that Job would have a better perspective on life if he viewed his predicament in the larger context of divine history. On that point he is right, though he fails to reveal to Job what that history may have meant.

Inquiring of bygone ages brings no true comfort. In fact, it may accentuate our feeling of loneliness. Shortly before his death, Francis Bacon reflected on his journey among his contemporaries and said: "My soul hath been a stranger in the course of my pilgrimage. I seem to have conversation among the ancients more than among those with whom I live." The same could be said of those who search for some safe anchor in the midst of angry seas. It is Job's fate to remain a stranger among friends, who can offer many logical propositions, but who themselves do not adopt their own advice to inquire of bygone ages.

History purifies the process of thinking and, thus, translates to us ideas of the past in more attractive forms. When the soul wanders among the ruins of traditional religion as Job knew it, then the mind either retreats or rebels. The pursuit of wisdom does not come to us naturally, nor do we always know to what end we should devote our lives. So we find our comfort and inspiration among those of the past who are no longer slaves to the multiple needs of material life. Their thoughts come to us liberated from the necessities we must still endure.

Conversation with the ancients saves us from the dilemmas of modern confusion. A cowardly attitude? Perhaps. Neither Job nor his friends have been able to produce ideas sufficiently powerful not to be in need of refinement. Ideas are seldom valid until they have been tested through many centuries of presence in the minds of people. But can Job afford the luxury of such a journey into the past?

History is capable of recognizing error and of producing its own purification and, through it, building a stronger foundation for truth. But like the friends of Job, we are too preoccupied by our own righteousness to seek truth for its own sake. Late in life we discover that those who are in no further need of vindication can become

. . . .

better guides for us as we reflect on the various stages of our journey through life. Cardinal Newman says, "Here below to live is to change, and to be perfect is to have changed often."

Job did not change often. The alteration of his life came brutally, as if he had crossed dark stormy clouds to discover that the world that had sustained him for so long had vanished, fallen into the night of despair. Could he find relief by invoking the spiritual presence of those who lived in the past and who may have the keys that could open the prison of his confinement?

Perhaps in his anxiety and rebellion Job hears a message whose words belong to the universal voice of humankind, but have now become inaudible. Somewhere along the journey the divine *logos* lost its power, and we often believe it was more evident and meaningful in the past. Bildad's advice is cogent, though perhaps for the wrong reasons. Bygone ages still contain a wisdom which could help us in our journey if we seek to avoid dangers we could not detect on our own.

During a recent visit to Europe, I lingered in the old Roman amphitheater of Nîmes (Arènes de Nîmes). There I lost all notion of time and found myself locked in the amphitheater after closing hours. The actual dilemma of finding a way out of my predicament clashed with my spiritual and intellectual journey back in time. My interest in what happened two millennia ago made my temporary predicament seem almost inconsequential. Present and past clash in ways that are not always easy to sort out. (Fortunately, I could slip out later through the stage door as singers filed in for a rehearsal of *Turandot*.)

One of the privileges I cherish is to have lived for many years in several millennia-old cities of Europe.

. . . .

There the inquiry into bygone ages never ceases. I especially remember the formative years of my professional life in Strasbourg where I met an elderly person who was to become a life-long friend. He knew every detail of every place, every building, every street, and every event and never tired of sharing his knowledge with friends. Through him we could discover times that would have remained unknown to us. When I visited with him for the last time, he simply let his hands fall as if to say, "There is much more we could speak about. But my time has come to an end." With his death we were deprived of the intimate knowledge no one else had of the past.

Now, technology has placed at our disposal countless resources and books containing the cultural treasures of history. We can linger in museums and retrace the great moments of peoples who lived before us. But there is something unique in the kind of knowledge anchored in a special soul. There were things my friend could not communicate to me. Similarly, there were aspects of Job's experience his friends could never understand. Each generation has left behind part of its mysteries for us to ponder, and each generation has taken to its grave secrets we shall never recover. We are fated to live with the ignorance of treasures bygone ages can no longer translate to us. The quest, however, must go on.

Bildad's suggestion rests on a simple proposition: God cannot distort justice or mistreat the righteous. Yet, the only proof he has of that is his own view of history and his conviction that time erodes every possibility for us to remain just and righteous. Truth is somehow hidden in the wisdom of those who lived before us. Bildad got hold of an important key to an understanding of Job's plight. Homer conveyed the same message through

. . . .

Odysseus' travel to the underworld. It might become unwise for Odysseus to proceed in life without the warnings of Agamemnon or the insights of the prophet Tiresias. So here too, Bildad begs Job to consider his plight not as a specific momentary phenomenon, but as a piece of the puzzle of human life. The present must always be enlightened by the events of the past, for wisdom was greater then than now.

The picture, however, cannot come together, for the piece of the puzzle representing Job does not fit anywhere within the pattern. The counsel of Bildad, though wise and cogent, cannot solve what is beyond human control. Eternity as well as time are distorted, and God seems to pervert justice, at least in the traditional way it is understood on the human scene. Where are the representatives of the past whom Job could turn to in order to understand his own situation? Bildad is right. There was more righteousness in the past for the simple reason that the universe appeared less complex. It is progress and success which brought misfortune to Job.

Satan is intent on winning his wager with God. In this specific case, time can no longer illuminate the situation, because it is unique. In our quest for redemption, God discloses to us eternal images and archetypes influenced neither by history nor progress. Bildad's advice to Job to inquire of bygone ages should have included those aspects of divine history which in fact do not belong to a human conception of time, past or present.

MEDITATION 22.

Contending with God. (Job 9:1-12)

he dejected Job full of sores, speaking from the ash pit of desolation, could not foresee that he was destined to become the universal companion of those who, in all ages, would wander through the injustices and hardships of earthly existence. His words conveyed the feeling of insignificance that has overtaken sufferers in search of divine reassurance: "How can a man be just before God? If one wishes to contend with him, one could not answer him once in a thousand times."

Even the small world of desolation to which Job had been confined was too vast for his mind to grasp. There was nothing left for Job but to acknowledge humbly that all efforts at vindication would remain unfulfilled. There simply could be no effective way of enticing God to abrogate suffering.

Ever since the expulsion of Adam and Eve from the garden of divine protection and solicitude, survival has been imperiled by the dual principle of exclusion and separation. Having become like God through the knowledge of good and evil, man and woman had to be excluded from divine eternity. They could not be allowed to live forever and eternally frustrate the purpose of the creator.

The exclusion from the garden meant separation from God, achieved by imposing on man and woman hard labor, misery, suffering, and death. In all of this, the way was open for a perpetual and unavoidable contention

. . . .

between creature and creator. Job knows there is no other way but to contend with God, even when one is fated to lose with a score of one thousand to one. Everything under the sun is in contention with divine decrees.

At Peniel, Jacob wrestled with the angel of the Lord. He won part of the battle and he obtained his blessing, but he was permanently wounded, the price for contending with God. The road from Peniel to anywhere else could be traveled only by limping from place to place, a powerful parable of the human condition.

Job was too exhausted to wrestle with Yahweh. He had been thrown down from the mountain peaks of success to abject misery, and for a time he questioned whether any debate with God was even possible. The sojourner of the land of Uz could not help but wonder whether the spiritual world he had known was still in existence. It took time before he realized that a new spiritual dimension had arisen, unacceptable to his wife, inscrutable to his friends, mysterious to himself.

In God's infinity, the particular situations of Jacob and Job transcended the quests they happened to be involved in. We all belonged with them in the desolation of the night or in the suffering of the ash pit. They achieved for us what we could not secure for ourselves. We were and are included vicariously in their struggle, doubt, failure, victory, or defeat. They atoned for us all the deeds we failed to perform for ourselves, for too many of us would not even know where to begin to contend with God in order to receive our blessing or survive in the midst of incredible spiritual and moral dearth.

God had chosen servants such as Jacob or Job to represent humanity in its suffering and quest. Our sense

. . . .

of isolation can make God imperceptible. In his despair Jeremiah complained, "I looked on the earth, and lo, it was waste and void; and to the heavens, and they had no light." Jeremiah knew that no one is as alone in the universe as the servant of God who must speak and cannot be heard.

Against all odds, Job became a giant of the faith, an unfortunate presence amid unfortunate events, a servant of God who dared revolt against the principles of exclusion and separation, a contender who knew that one does not argue with God, yet is entitled to beg for participation in a process intent on excluding him without cause from all that had been dear to him. As an exhausted pilgrim in an exhausted world, he had no choice but to acknowledge defeat without ever abandoning the battle. He knew then, as we know now, that we contend with God every day, even as we through faith remain in the divine circle of compassion.

. . . .

MEDITATION 23.

"Though I am innocent, my own mouth would condemn me."
(Job 9:20)

estined to move in a world that appeared void of happiness and virtue, Job grew accustomed to contemplating everything from the point of view of its objective existence. Like him, we come to perceive great truths without grasping their importance, without establishing the connections to the greater and larger contexts of divine purpose. The God who makes his presence available to us never compels us to avail ourselves of it. It remains our responsibility to determine how much we can elevate ourselves above the deadening events that beset our temporal pilgrimage.

Creating our own sense of the universal and the spiritual does not come naturally to us, for we do not have within ourselves the resources to help us overcome the burdens of everyday life. Like Job, we may feel condemned even within our feeling of innocence, for how do we define innocence in a context that belies any possibility of peace of heart and peace of mind? How do we grasp for a moment what comes from nowhere and goes on to nowhere?

We hear the elusive call to let our beings be filled with the divine invisible force animating the world, yet faith fails us, for our natural self does not possess the qualities of eternity and permanence. Yet eternity begins here on earth and God has given the invitation not to let life escape our control in spite of apparent absurdities.

. . . .

Every day we pass judgment on our lives, either in a positive or negative fashion. Every day we condemn ourselves to life or to death, for when we fail to add a touch of the divine spirit to our endeavors, life flees from us into nothingness. Much too often we miss the opportunity to endow our fleeting moments with permanent worth, for we fail to penetrate the divine within us. In what we speak, in what we do, in what we feel, in what we give, in every aspect, we experience the urge toward something greater. Yet we also feel a pervasive sense of failure as we realize how little of the essential we are able to grasp. When poets and playwrights praise the wonderful qualities of being human, do they realize how difficult it is to discover those wonders within us?

As for Job, everything pointed toward his condemnation, which he was incapable of forming any argument against. Wisdom had left the scene. To whom could he protest his innocence? His words were few, though spoken in indignation, anger, and frustration. And in all of that, God refused to grant him the touch of the spirit that could have enlightened his situation.

In the beginning God spoke his creative word, and the universe came into existence to give shape and form to that word. It was beautiful and bore the mark of the eternal. It was predestined to repeat itself and move to higher and higher levels of divine fulfillment. Then came our word, which held the power to annihilate heaven's gift, a *logos* reduced to self-interest, the weapon of rebellion, yet a word God must acknowledge, for it still resembles the divine *logos*. Job's protest of innocence can no longer be formulated from within the divine *logos*. It is to be affirmed with human words, hence the perennial feeling of inadequacy and guilt.

. . . .

MEDITATION 24.

"Would that there were an umpire between us." (Job 9:33)

he conflict between God and Job cannot be subjected to human norms of justice and righteousness. The unerring divine mind cannot accept any blame. Thus, we are always guilty, though possibly innocent. Job has learned how to accept such a reality, however depressing. In the presence of God, silence and submission alone are acceptable. Mortals do not question God. Time does not contend with eternity. Job has now put two pieces of the puzzle together with the most discouraging result. He affirms his innocence while loathing his life. The consciousness of innocence destroys the content of life. Who, but Job, could understand such perplexity?

In front of God, Job has lost all rights. The existence of ultimate justice which rewards proper conduct is here summarily defeated. God alone can act without cause and not be accountable.

At one point Erasmus questioned the position of Luther that grace alone and not works can save us. Under such a principle, argued Erasmus, who would take the trouble to lead a good life? Who could justify a God whose principle is caprice? To that Luther answered, "It is the supreme expression of faith to think Him merciful who saves so few, and condemns so many; to think Him just, who of His own will has made us of necessity damnable, so that, as Erasmus says, it seems that He takes pleasure in the tortures of the unfortunate, and is worthy rather of hatred than love. If by any reason I could understand how

. . . .

this God, who shows so much evil and wrath, could be merciful, then I should have no need of faith."

Job's wish that there were a scale on which the actions of God and mortals could be weighed comes from the genuine conviction that there must be a harmony between divine will and human obedience to it. Great is his indignation when he realizes that the creator of the universe is the author of principles to which he himself does not have to submit, for he will always be greater than what proceeds from him.

Job is progressively moving to a conclusion that might endanger the moral structure of reality. Since there is no correlation between innocence and divine approbation, moral and ethical behavior might end up in naught. We labor in vain toward any kind of moral imperative. Morality implies a common bond uniting its source and its effect. Where God removes himself as a source, the effects no longer matter, and there is scarcely a distinction between the just and the wicked. Thus God, in the same breath, can mock the calamity of the innocent and deliver the earth into the hand of the wicked.

Job, however, knows that we are ill equipped to discriminate between the positive and the negative, and they often appear to us as the contrary of what they essentially are. Our criteria of evaluation lack the perspective of eternity because things as we know them are contained within time. So, we must transcend our rationality, and sometimes abandon it, in order to enter a divine mode of understanding. Knowledge born out of wisdom is rare, though when present it redirects our wishes and purposes in unexpected ways. As Heraclitus suggests, if we feel uncomfortable with the unexpected, we should not seek to know the truth.

. . . .

Does Job really need an umpire, an arbiter, or a middle man? He has lived through enough agony to form his personal view of a world that baffles those who appear within it. How special is he in the eyes of his Lord? Every day brings with it either an increase or a diminution in the blessings we enjoy. Every day witnesses the death of so much that is dear to us, and every day new life and hope spring to comfort us in our distress. Moment after moment in our earthly pilgrimage we have to learn anew how to grow into happiness while our spiritual being is lost in what is greater than ourselves.

Nobel Prize winning biochemist Jacques Monod wrote about the awesome responsibility that overcomes us as we discover our position in the scheme of life: "Man at last knows that he is alone in the unfeeling immensity of the universe. Neither his destiny nor his duty have been written down. It is for him to choose between the kingdom and darkness." Has not Job vaccilated between the kingdom and darkness to the extent that we find him in close communion with his Lord or in rebellion against anything God may have intended?

When God allows us to be pushed to the extremes of our ability, and when we are forced to choose between what enhances life and what diminishes it, then we too might wish for a mediator who could infuse in us a sense of reassurance by proving us right. At many points life compels us to contend with God, even when we are ignorant of the rules of the game or the purpose of the struggle. The plea of Job may become our own.

Strangely enough, righteousness remains imperative for Job, but no longer as a means to satisfy God, rather as an affirmation that he can bring into existence his own justice and, so to speak, force God to validate it.

. . . .

Since God cannot be bound to accept human innocence, despair can be averted by the persistent effort to contrive a way of life that even God cannot reject. Was Job becoming more than he should be in the eyes of God? Possibly so. To wish to be the judge of God's actions in the same way God is the judge of human actions goes beyond biblical religion. But so does Job.

. . . .

MEDITATION 25.

"Let me alone, that I may find a little comfort." (Job 10:20)

hen the bonds of creation were broken, when God himself relinquished part of his work to the adversary, then Job found no choice but to retreat within himself and search for a religious consciousness which sprang from his own being. Having now entered a world alien to him, Job repeated his dismay at the fact that birth never takes into account our powerlessness.

Rationality becomes a liability when it can no longer connect with a divine source. The lot of mortals is continuous vexation, a journey from understanding to doubt, from order to chaos. If there is any comfort, it must be self-made and come from the depth of anguish, from the ability to rise from the abyss to the light of day.

We find in the Book of Job many prayers that convey a deep sense of loneliness. "Let me alone," when addressed to God, can hardly be a request in line with our basic search for divine protection and providence. Perhaps we try too hard to reorder the natural and spiritual world over which we seem to exercise an illusory authority. The balance is not easy to achieve.

On the one hand, we seek a genuine unity with the divine, believing that God has made us participants in the universal drama of life. On the other hand, we seek to assert our individuality and to form our personalities in the image of what we conceive to be the ultimate good for ourselves. Our plight is that our knowledge never

. . . .

reaches any level of purity, since we are fated from the beginning to partake of uncertainties. When we ignore this duality, we enter into a dangerous zone where even divine gifts can be transformed into destructive elements.

Job no longer believes that God intends to vindicate justice by meting out fair and acceptable portions. True comfort can come only from solitariness: "Let me alone that I may find a little comfort." Job's request for solitariness springs from deep religious intuition. It is not a quest for God's absence, but for the discovery of the awesome side of God's creation which escapes us in the business of life or when we are unduly preoccupied with our individual destiny. Wordsworth writes, "When from our better selves we have too long been parted by the hurrying world, and droop, sick of its business, of its pleasures tired, how gracious, how benign, is solitude."

Often we find ourselves at the crossroads of uncertainty and do not know which way to go. Goethe suggested that two souls live in our breasts, each trying to reach a goal different from the other one. Without any specific design, it is the better self that suffers the most. Yet solitude is necessary, for it creates moral, intellectual, and spiritual power. We must occasionally step out of ourselves in order to understand better the forces at work in our lives. Solitude may mean getting acquainted with our multiple selves, our multiple wishes, and our multiple destinies.

From the beginning loneliness became part of life, and it will remain with us till the end of conscious existence. It emerges from the vast realm of the unknown, from the feeling of being lost in the immensity of the universe. For that reason, most of us will never feel totally at home in the cosmos, for we shall never come to know it in its forbidding infinity.

. . . .

Anxiety comes from the lack of communion between what and who we are and the purpose of a universe we fail to fathom. Some things are not for us to know, for indeed they cannot be known. Even amid greatness, some giants of the human race have experienced and sometimes welcomed solitude. Einstein writes, "I am truly a 'lone traveler' and have never belonged to my country, my home, my friends, or even my immediate family, with my whole heart; in the face of all these ties, I have never lost a sense of distance and a need for solitude—feelings which have increased with the years. One becomes sharply aware, but without regret, of the limits of mutual understanding and consonance with other people. No doubt, such a person loses some of his innocence and unconcern; on the other hand, he is largely independent of the opinions, habits, and judgments of his fellows and avoids the temptation to build his inner equilibrium upon such insecure foundations." We find the same attitude in Job, mostly when he gets exasperated by the advice of his friends and family.

But dare we find in ourselves what we can no longer find in God? When the original equilibrium is lost, who can rebuild it? Job must assume the plight of loneliness and transform it into a life-giving possibility. He may not find much in his own resigned state of mind; but however little he finds there seems better than what God has so far allowed him to have.

If to fall in the hands of the living God is a terrible thing, then maybe we should avoid being there. Is that what Job feels at the moment? He pleads with God to forsake him and give him the temporary hope of a little comfort not threatened by divine whim. He knows that there is no permanence in such comfort, but just the fleeting experience of it might give him a reason to believe in its eternal existence. The perspective of death will abrogate any hope of lasting comfort. But is it asking for too much when Job begs for a little self-made comfort before entering the land of gloom from which there is no return?

Job reviews the reasons for his misfortune. He loathes his life because it lacks unity and harmony. The dialectic of blessing and rejection continues to rule over him, for the God who creates can also destroy. Job remains aware of the fragility of life: "Thy hands fashioned and made me; and now thou dost turn about and destroy me." Yet Job is determined to pursue and find God's purpose even in the midst of fear. He pleads with God to consider human frailty: "Remember that thou hast made me of clay; and wilt thou turn me to dust again?" However threatened our existence may become, the story of Job reminds us that there are blessings which belong to God's eternity and will accompany us for ever, though our temporary afflictions may hide them from us.

Perhaps in eternity, when suffering will no longer rule, God will allow us to keep some pleasant memory of what little well-being we were able to introduce into our earthly lives. Our comfort will no longer come from solitude. None of us, not even Job, will have to pray again, "Let me alone." Beyond the land of gloom, our hope of divine presence will acquire the status of the universal. It will belong to the fellowship of the redeemed when the sum total of our experiences will belong to all. Neither Job nor we can easily entertain such a faith while struggling with the hardships of the moment.

. . . .

MEDITATION 26.

"Know then that God exacts of you less than your guilt deserves." (Job 11:6)

Zophar tries to keep things in perspective. The survival of the sinner depends on mercy, not justice. He intends to teach Job that his claim to innocence rests on an erroneous view of life. Job, he thinks, has crossed the line of propriety by imputing wrong motives to God and expecting from him more than he deserves. He has, so to speak, become too conscious of his own importance. Somehow, faith in God should lead us away from an undue preoccupation with ourselves, for the end of religion is communion with God.

In his relationship to us, God maintains perfection, and we must submit to his will. Spiritual reassurance comes from the hope that God does not mete out punishment according to the gravity of our sin. In his compassion, God never operates on the level of sheer justice, a principle which would prove fatal to all.

But does any of this apply to Job? Does Zophar know why God is contending with him? Job did not formulate the wager between God and Satan. Not much is within his power, and his mind wanders over the landscape filled with disasters, none of them of his own making. For the moment, Job's God seems to have turned his anger toward his creation, as if it were no longer his work.

Zophar tries to comfort Job by reminding him that God exacts less than his guilt deserves. He has based his message on beliefs that could be upheld by most religious people, but which, in this particular instance, reveal a fundamental ignorance of God's will. A knowledge of divine expectations might threaten religious comfort and security for the simple reason that God most often does not disclose to us the details of his purpose. No collective dogma or religious belief can properly address our personal communion with God, however much or little of it becomes clear to us. It is our normal tendency to seek understanding and to try to penetrate divine decrees concerning us. When faith no longer provides the necessary anchors, we seek answers in rational questioning. But we ought to remember the warning of the wise preacher: "He who increases knowledge will increase sorrow."

The voice of reason often leads to oversimplification. Zophar has developed a system of thought he believes to be flawless. If Job can set his heart aright and remove iniquity and wickedness from his life, he will find peace and wholeness again. But somehow perfect solutions refuse to fit an imperfect world. Zophar's insight into heavenly powers is so rudimentary that he could not comprehend the nature of the wager being tested. Our spiritual comfort may require that we be spared coming too close to God. The friends of Job have learned their lessons well, and they recite their beliefs with conviction. Their speech is forceful, often convincing. They are able to lay Job's guilt at his own feet. But they certainly cannot bridge the gap separating their thinking and the will of God. God does not readily reveal himself to those who feel comfortable within their religious beliefs.

The assumption that we possess the ability to restore the pieces of the puzzle to their proper place may in fact blind us to the reality of a broken creation in search of healing. Certainly God exacts less from us than our guilt deserves. But, like Job, we find ourselves in situations where we have not been the architects of our affliction. We may never comprehend why our redemption must include our participation in the struggle affecting the totality of creation. Zophar can find comfort in his theology. Job, however, has come to know the true meaning of existence.

There are two basic ways to look at God. We could attach a spiritual meaning to every dimension of our relationship to the divinity. In humility, we should acknowledge divine superiority and human dependence. In such a situation we are always at fault, whatever the circumstances. God rules supreme over creation, and, through his providence, dispenses the grace necessary for its survival.

But there is also another way to look at God—Job's way. It is the way of argument, of questioning, of doubting, and of rebelling. In such a perspective God need not always be right, and his ways with us, though unavoidable, need not be acceptable. Zophar refuses to extend religious thought that far. No one wants to incur the blame of irreverence or faithlessness.

Zophar's hope is that God will eventually reveal his wisdom to Job. In fact God has, but Zophar could not know it. He represents the average religious person intent on giving God his due without questioning his actions. But when a well-balanced religious world collapses, as in Job's case, answers to our human condition no longer exist. They must be recreated out of the debris we no longer understand, hidden in some mysterious divine *telos,* which may or may not correspond to any of our yearnings. If God exacts less than his due, how could he expect Job to give him more than he owes?

MEDITATION 27.

"Wisdom is with the aged, and understanding in length of days." (Job 12:12)

n praise of old age! Maturity brings us closer to immortality and consequently to God. The elusive wisdom which retreats from youthful impulsiveness finally makes its home in our tamed hearts and minds. When the needs of the physical body diminish, the soul experiences a sense of liberation. The mechanical machine of bones and flesh can and will suffer fatigue and exhaustion, but it cannot pull the soul down with it. The most judicious and intense perspectives on life come with the prospect of death. That which will no longer be loses importance, and that which will remain forever takes form and shape in the intellect and the soul.

God deprived Job of his earthly goods and created a high level of indignation in the name of fairness and justice. But did Job know that wisdom has a home of its own, a home which cannot be made ready except after years of preparation? It takes many long days to recognize what should have always been there.

If Ecclesiastes is right in asserting that there is a time for everything, when is the time for wisdom? Wisdom belongs to the state of reflection, to the fulfilled life no longer subjected to the urges and vanities we welcome in our younger years. Wisdom comes to us when we no longer stand in need of anything, when life can finally be experienced for its own sake and not in view of anything else. That can come to us only after years of experience, with the simplicity of being and the integrity of knowing oneself at peace with the process of aging.

. . . .

None of this, however, means that the young cannot be chosen by God to mediate learning and blessings. Timothy had been the victim of rejection by elders and took comfort in Paul's advice: "Let no one despise your youth, but set the believers an example in speech and conduct, in love, in faith, in purity." Later in the story of Job, we meet an impulsive young contender who wishes to assert his perspective as more valid than those of older friends by stating, "It is not the old that are wise, nor the aged that understand what is right."

There is, in fact, a Russian proverb which correlates wisdom with experience rather than length of life: "Ask not the aged, ask him who knows about life." Tolstoy may have had that in mind when he wrote his stirring story called *The Death of Ivan Ilyich*. Though different from the story of Job, there are striking similarities in both accounts.

The story of Ivan Ilyich is one of the simplest yet most tragic stories of literature. Though not notoriously special, Ivan Ilyich was an ordinary, obedient citizen whose goal was to lead a peaceful and successful life. By playing the game according to the rules he received his promotions in his work. Soon he realized his dream of being able to afford a comfortable apartment, a luxury not often achieved in his day. While redecorating the apartment and hanging curtains, he fell and hurt himself. Slowly but pervasively the process of dying has entered his life.

Ivan Ilyich fell like Job from success to tragedy, and like Job he had friends who tried to comfort him, though they were unable to assess his situation correctly. Ivan's life no longer conformed to anything logical. He had finally become himself, yet a mystery to others. It was from the perspective of death that he began to realize what life should have been.

. . . .

Ivan came to know that advancement in his work and the possession of an apartment were illusory symbols of happiness. While seeking worldly success, he saw neither the sun nor the stars. He noticed nothing of importance, though it was all around him. Only in the perspective of death did he understand that he failed to perceive the real meaning of life. His neighbors and friends reasoned with the stoic wisdom of an Epictetus. But he himself recognized that the existing order would not be upset by his early departure.

If wisdom comes with age, it also dies with those who are its repository. Job had to concede the point: "No doubt you are the people, and wisdom will die with you." The friends and relatives of Ivan Ilyich could not comprehend his unfortunate situation, and the friends of Job concluded that wisdom had left the scene. In their loneliness and misfortune, both Ivan and Job were regarded as guilty individuals who, for some unclear reason, had betrayed God and society.

Still Job claims innocence and wisdom. He refuses to be identified with evildoers who achieve success in life, but not in the eyes of God. To his friends he says, "But I have understanding as well as you; I am not inferior to you. . . . I am a laughingstock to my friends; I, who called upon God and he answered me." Job proceeds to show that wisdom is not with the successful, but written in big letters everywhere within God's creation, at least for those who have eyes to see.

Wisdom no longer seeks either vindication or justification. It accepts life as it comes and understands it in the light of eternal being. Perhaps the most difficult lesson for us to accept is that material needs, to the extent that they dominate our lives, preclude the possibility of wisdom. When our wants become few, life can be experienced more fully, undistracted by the vanity of useless things. Augustine liked to say, "What a shame to know and to possess so many things, and yet to know oneself so little." The journey inward begins later in life when, at the cost of anguish and anxiety, we learn how to shut out the material world.

To experience life in its fullest also means to be able to silence distracting voices and prejudices. The religious person knows, without being able to explain it, that present existence must be superseded by a calm, peaceful, and serene contemplation. Even as participants in this world of chaos, our lives can acquire worth and eternity. There must be a culmination beyond the process of formation, where reflection crosses over to wisdom, where worship finds its long sought for reward, and where God's presence replaces our yearnings for it.

How ironic that we should come to know at the dusk of life when knowledge seems no longer necessary! But precisely because it is not necessary, it can be experienced in its purest form as poetry itself, as beauty realized. If virtue has its own reward, so does wisdom when it is no longer reduced to the role of servant of our needs and when it can free the mind from dangerous assumptions. In his later years, Socrates reflected on the fact that "as we grow older, the spiritual eye becomes keen when the corporeal eyes begin to lose their sharpness." To that, one of his guests replied, "I would have you know that, for my part, as the satisfactions of the body decay, the more I welcome the charm and pleasure of good conversation."

God never intended for us to *own* things, only to be guests within his creation. Job has finally learned that

. . . .

God can give and take away, and still remain God. Conversely, we can gain or lose and still remain fully human. Wisdom connects the two propositions by teaching us how to bring the right perspective to our material needs while not neglecting the harmony of what remains forever.

MEDITATION 28.

"Let me have silence." (Job 13:13)

isdom requires but a few words. Language is one of the most powerful divine gifts but often misused and sometimes dangerous. While our words may convey genuine intentions, they remain open to misunderstanding. Job appears ungrateful for the advice his friends have so relentlessly offered. And therein lies the unacceptable burden. Having spoken too much, they also revealed the futility of their speeches: "Your maxims are proverbs of ashes, your defenses are defenses of clay."

By what standards is Job evaluating the intentions of his friends? Are they guilty of dethroning the *logos,* the divine word, in favor of slogans and platitudes? Or have they come to realize that those who try to convey their feelings and concerns know the deep sense of inadequacy that can overcome them when their words cannot be joined to their thoughts? That wisdom resides more in silence than in speech does not appear to us as an acceptable proposition, for we are persuaded that language is our best weapon for self-justification.

But what do words convey? Certainly not the depth of our beings, for our very essence cannot be expressed to others. There is a side to our lives that remains so deeply personal it would be destroyed in our attempt to communicate it. Job experiences this excruciating paradox about the power of words when he feels compelled to speak, to reprove his friends, to plead with God, to protest his unfair predicament. Yet he also knows that the words he speaks cannot convey the depth of his feelings. The most dedicated servants of God have often felt the greatest anguish of solitude and have opted for long periods of silence.

Before Job can speak, he must secure the silence of those around him, a silence that means peace of heart and mind. It requires solitude and inner concentration.

How many words do we need in order to let God know who we are? Life bears witness to itself, and what we say about it neither enhances nor diminishes its value. No speech of Job or his friends could alter the divine decrees in a wager made in heaven. Yet words are necessary to share with each other what is important to all. But too many words lead to foolishness. Abundance turns to mediocrity.

Words are by nature creative, whether on the side of evil or the side of goodness. Therefore, they should be used judiciously both as a means of exchange and as the interpretation of our feelings, emotions, and passions. The error of Job's friends was that they believed they had insight into his plight. They tried to impose their perspectives on a situation that escaped them. They assumed that they could be God's representatives at a time when God chose to be silent. In any spiritual vacuum, God's word is supplanted by human words. What does it take to reach the conviction that we speak in God's name? Can anyone ever reach that point and become God's prophet amid human chaos?

A sense of righteousness about our religious commitments does not make them correct. How then can we reach the unalterable realm of truth? Certainly not in what we say. It is not for us to endow words with meaning.

. . . .

They come to us with their own power, a power that most of the time eludes us. We feel more comfortable by reducing them to our level than by rising to their divine content. Only God can speak his creativity and bring the world into existence by the power of words, and those words are few. So, why should ours be so many?

When the soul finally learns how to be in spiritual communion with its maker, it also knows how to listen to the silence of the spheres. Day and night the heavens proclaim the glory of God in a divine speech not audible to our ears. No matter how relentless the tribulations, Job does not relinquish the hope of finding within God's creation the healing power of silence. Perhaps God could speak to his troubled soul without using words. Max Picard reflects on the awesomeness of silence in writing:

> Silence reveals itself in a thousand inexpressible forms: in the quiet of dawn, in the noiseless aspiration of trees towards the sky, in the stealthy descent of night, in the silent changing of the seasons, in the falling moonlight, trickling down into the night like a rain of silence, but above all in the silence of the inward soul—all these forms of silence are nameless: all the clearer and surer is the word that arises out of and in contrast to the nameless silence.

There is a *logos* which reaches the end of the world, whether or not we can discern it or make room for it in our being. That which we cannot hear may still convey to us divine eloquence as it is made manifest in God's handiwork.

In heaven only a few words are necessary because perfection is in no need of defense or argument. Here on earth we have to fight our limitations through the proliferation of speech. Though he doesn't know it, Job

. . . .

finds himself between heaven and earth, feeling the weight of his physical misery, while entertaining religious intuitions seldom granted to mortals. He found the connection between grief and silence and, thus, could alleviate the burden of his life. He also spoke, and his speech was angry, bold, and passionate. His voice still echoes through the empty spaces of life. With him we speak, and with him we listen, and we learn the most when we contemplate in silence what God has chosen not to reveal to us until our hearts and minds find their peace in the harmony of all things, beyond good and evil.

MEDITATION 29.

"Only grant two things to me . . . withdraw thy hand far from me, and let not dread of thee terrify me." (Job 13:20–21)

nder blows he has suffered so far, Job could no longer estimate what his relationship to God should be. What kind of prayer could he still formulate that would reach heaven? At times he is overwhelmed by God's oppressive presence. At other times he feels that the infinite spaces separating him from his creator are frighteningly empty and forbidding.

When life lay ruined by divine design, what could be uttered with equanimity? And how could one still trust in divine providence? Religion's function is to reassure mortals of God's benevolence. But Job voices a resolute wish to be removed from the presence of God and to experience the peace of silence.

Since Job neither created nor controls the circumstances of life, he does not wish to know either their source or their end. Job's closeness to God precludes serenity and tranquility. The creator who dispenses blessings can also reduce existence to affliction. Certainly Job does not expect to subdue circumstances to his will or to command them another destiny than the one divinely ordained. Yet, he would have wanted to rule sufficiently over his life to penetrate some of its mysteries.

Divine governance, when in conflict with human understanding, possesses neither compassion nor rationality. Long after Job's story was told, Epictetus, a Roman slave abused by his master and permanently injured, became a leading exponent of stoic philosophy. He, too,

. . . .

lamented the lack of rationality and justice in a world of ignorance and brutality. His prayer was in a way similar to and in other ways different from Job's. He did not wish for God's remoteness. But he pleaded with the divinity to grant him the wisdom to accept the things over which he had no power.

It is our natural inclination to devise religious ways which attenuate the awe and mystery of God's presence. We protect ourselves by relying on the superficiality of our spiritual worlds. When tragedy occurs, the inner resources are lacking, for divine presence is not what human beings desire. In his misery, Job knows that God has the power to annihilate our religious convictions.

In the presence of God, we become conscious of our transitoriness. Divine perfection, to the extent that we are capable of surmising it, stands in opposition to our mortality. The remoteness of God is not only a reality; it may also become our wish. The Old Testament prophets were scorned and persecuted because they proclaimed God's proximity to the extent that it destroyed the comfortable practices of formal religion. There was more peace in God's remoteness than in his presence. Job reached the same conclusion. He knew that in the vernacular of his day the people used the same word *paqad* to denote God's visit and God's punishment. The one almost automatically engendered the other.

In the case of Job, God's intermediary is also his adversary, and Job is left with no choice or escape. God's people of old did not attempt to solve the inconsistencies in their religious intuition. Like the Psalmist, Job had accepted the inescapability of God's universal rule. There is no place to retreat from God's spirit or to flee from his presence.

. . . .

Job came close to wishing he could live in a reality removed from God's burdensome dominion. The turmoil that afflicts nature also mirrors God's intention not to let us forget our precarious status within creation: "The mountain falls and crumbles away, and the rock is removed from its place; the waters wear away the stones; the torrents wash away the soil of the earth; so thou destroyest the hope of man. Thou prevailest for ever against him, and he passes."

Divine memory contains all the great and petty sins Job cannot dismiss. There is no relief when facing an eternity full of human aberrations. Hope of progressing in life is achieved at the cost of putting some distance between God and us. For Job, it becomes his prayer, a genuine and intense one, a realization that one does not survive in a divinely ordered reality. Job knows that he can neither comprehend nor accept the chaos which plagues creation and threatens his relationship to God. Divine order remains elusive.

The terrifying experience of Job does not come from the fact that he has lost everything. He is much more at sea when he tries to penetrate the meaning of a baffling divine wager. His faith clashes with his new notion of divine justice and providence. Creation no longer mirrors divine excellence, but divine inability to eliminate or even reduce the power of so many leviathans keeping everything in a state of chaos.

Job recognizes that he is the author of his misery, but he no longer can estimate the end assigned to his life. Has divine providence become so negative that Job should wish to be spared from it? Should he not rather wish, like Epicurus, that the gods should remain happy in their eternal home and not interfere with life on earth? Job is

. . . .

not ready for such an abdication. All he wants now is a certain distance from God so he can face with courage the reality of being human.

We shall never discover why God chose to place us in the midst of uncertainties. The closer we come to any understanding, the more evident the conflicts of the heart, mind, and soul. Knowledge, as God may have intended it for us, can only reveal the heart in conflict with itself, the mind roaming through the debris of life, and the soul yearning for what should have been its due all along. Thus, we hesitate, for the road ahead will contain all the reminders of our transitoriness, perhaps to the point that we too might be led to choose neutrality in the hope that it might spare us from a divine presence too awesome for us to bear.

. . . .

MEDITATION 30.

"Wilt thou frighten a driven leaf and pursue dry chaff?" (Job 13:25)

ob's relative position in a cosmos that appears to be indifferent to his presence leads him to gravitate between two baffling propositions—one allowing him to partake of the realm of the wonderful, the other reducing him to nothingness.

Job carries in his being the divine image reflecting the purpose of God. Yet, as soon as he allows himself even a minimal examination of his position in the world, he is overwhelmed by a tragic sense of insignificance, for nothing can close the gap separating him from his creator. His imperative is not to lose faith. As the King James version renders Job's words, "Though he slay me, yet will I trust in him." Yet faith demands a strong sense of identity: "Yet I will defend my ways to his face."

Job realizes that the outcome of his destiny is not a foregone conclusion and that his confrontation with his creator might bring more vexation to his life and to his sense of selfhood than he can successfully overcome. His request for justification represents a Sisyphean attempt. The higher he pushes the boulder up the mountain, the farther he falls. Thus, there is little hope to come face to face with a creator who intends for him to remain aware of his status and position in the realm of divine rule. Good and evil, time and eternity, death and immortality clash in ways beyond the grasp of the mind; existence remains threatened by fundamental contradictions.

. . . .

Not so long ago the driven, wind-blown leaf was the prized jewel in God's crown: "Have you considered my servant Job, that there is none like him on the earth, a blameless and upright man." At one time infinitely great, at another time infinitely small, how could Job ever make sense of God's economy for a creation in turmoil? From angels to beasts, from creatures bearing God's image to sinners to be removed from God's presence, we must travel the roads of uncertainty on a divine map never disclosing any precise destination. The author of Ecclesiastes warns us that God made everything beautiful and that he put the hope of eternity into our minds. But God also made sure that none of us would ever come to know what he has done from beginning to end. Why then are we so important in a universal scheme in which we remain of so little consequence? The Psalmist asks, "What is man that thou art mindful of him, and the son of man that thou dost care for him?" Then he answers, "An evening shadow."

Somewhere beyond the uncertainties of life are the horizons we could reach to receive answers to our troubling questions. But it is in the nature of horizons to retreat farther and farther as we approach them. Dismayed, Job contemplates a vanishing point toward which nothing converges any more. His existence reflects an amalgamation of fragments, pieces of a puzzle which simply would not fit together to form any acceptable picture. Perhaps by removing God from that picture there would still be hope. But hope without faith leads only to greater turmoil, and Job is determined to see the battle to the end, regardless of its outcome.

. . . .

As long as Job was a successful person, he did not have to raise too many questions about ultimate destiny. But when he no longer revolved within a secure world that he had constructed for himself, the question of existence was thrust upon him. He became painfully aware of the larger divine purpose he contemplated only from a safe distance. His search for himself made him aware of the oppressiveness of temporality. So much can develop in the drama of existence in so short a time that it could not make sense.

Job became a riddle to himself. What he understood to be a conflict with God was in fact a conflict with himself as a servant of God, chosen to bear witness to a higher world of spirituality without knowing it. There was so much more to Job's life than what he could feel, say, or even believe. It is in the nature of the bearers of great truths to be destroyed by the transcendent oppressiveness of those very truths.

The driven leaf and the dry chaff must come to see the center of being not in themselves but in God. The hyperconsciousness of Job makes his human condition unbearable because it does not properly relate to anything he can explain or understand. Within such a context, suffering keeps its dual aspect, as the consequence of sin and as the only way to redemption.

In suffering, as Paul suggests, we discover "the glorious liberty of the children of God." Without suffering there could be no spiritual being. On the road to redemption, all must confront tragedy in one way or another. There is no smooth transition from temporality to eternity, from life to immortality. After every thrust of thinking, Job has to accept the reality of his powerlessness and the incomprehensible concern of God.

. . . .

Because the driven leaves and the dry chaff possess divine elements, Job must learn that they are an integral part of creation and that God must redeem them for his creation to reach the stage of completeness. In the perspective of eternity, it matters very little whether we know the meaning of the roles we must play.

"Wilt thou frighten a driven leaf?" Yes! There is no way for us to live within God's creation and not experience the dread of threatened existence. In the case of Job the driven, wind-blown leaf becomes the companion traveling with us through the uncertainties of our earthly pilgrimage. He is the saint who lives his suffering and finds meaning in it. He is the prophet who proclaims what he feels God has infused into his life, leading either to joy or sorrow. He is the poet in search of what is not common to all. He is the epitome of Pascal's surmise: "You would not be searching for me, had you not already found me."

Having Job as our companion we discover that our feeling of separateness from God is the necessary first step toward redemption, for in it we find that the ineffable greatness of God already includes us. That, in itself, is sufficient to make us partake of a universal joy, while conscious of our unworthiness.

. . . .

MEDITATION 31.

"If a man die, shall he live again?" (Job 14:14)

ob's plea reflects a genuine quest for divine justice. Can a moral God withdraw life from us and not give it back? Life is always a trump card in God's hand, and we have no recourse against the ways that card is played. The futility of it all overpowers Job and sharpens his indignation.

Death places us outside of time. It destroys what in biblical language is called the *kairos,* or the divine time which allows us to discover God's purpose in the midst of human limitations. The *kairos* is extended to us so we can bring our lives in agreement with God's expectations. Job faced the struggle we all must enter as we attempt to assign to the flow of time an acceptable meaning. We live in two specific time dimensions. On the one hand, we are subjected to the *chronos,* the chronological time that ticks away with the movement of all clocks and is impervious to our relationship to it. It elapses whether we think or not, whether we sleep or not, whether we search for anything or not. The *kairos,* on the other hand, is the God-given opportunity to fill the *chronos* with meaning through judicious decisions. Often there is no second chance, as Jesus pointed out to unrepenting people. Job had his *kairos.* Jesus had his. And we have our own.

Job knew that his life was subject to more than chronological time. He looked for a *kairos* which could introduce to his endeavors a sense of rationality and fulfillment. Instead he had to accept the simple, though discouraging, proposition that the norms of justice do not determine his destiny. Our expectation to meet within divine creation the principles of coherence and harmony encounters only frustration when we fail to accept in humility that it is not in our power to assign meaning to any divine *kairos*. The *kairos* already contains an inalterable divine purpose that we must make real in our lives. The difficulty comes when we realize that creation does not exhibit its inner workings in terms of fairness. It is hard to accept that, even within a divine *kairos*, there are physical, moral, and spiritual battles we cannot win. After our present experiment on earth is over, will God grant us another opportunity to complete that which we left unfinished?

We cross life subjected to a destiny beyond our control. As beings of a few days, born to trouble and withering like flowers of a moment, we have no way to estimate what any occasion means within the scope of eternity. Our human condition compels us to see the succession of events as having a validity of their own. But it is not given to us to know what each instant represents in its connection to the universal.

We experience life in what seems an endless series of contradictions, and we often bemoan the fact that life is not treating us fairly. If death overtakes us before we come to taste life in its fullness, should we not be given an opportunity to live again and realize what escaped us during our short days on earth? Why shouldn't we partake of the privilege of the plant which, when cut down, has the possibility to sprout again?

Why, however, should Job want to come back to life if it is to experience the same frustrations? Does not sheol offer a better protection, a place where neither the divine nor the human rule, where neither can influence or

. . . .

destroy the other? Job would welcome that place of hiding, if for no other reason than to escape the wrath of God.

Job surmises that he will carry with him into Sheol a lifetime of misery, deprivation, and discontent. When all has ended in nothingness, we need no longer be conscious of worlds collapsing around us. How relative can things become! Mountains can crumble and rocks be removed from their place, torrents can work away the soil, and we can lose all hope. In the world of the unconscious it no longer matters. One can contemplate utter devastation without being affected by it anymore.

In Sheol one needs nothing, not even God, and for a moment Job considers such a possibility a real relief. In Sheol alone, as Job understood it, could there be a perfect exile from both God and the world. The journey from nothingness to nothingness becomes painful only when one forgets the origin and the destination. Job finds himself in the middle of things, of what never was in his power. He cannot find peace because there never was any voluntary acceptance of events he did not control.

For a time, there was no joy in Job's awareness that he has come face to face with a universal and enduring reality. Instead of finding comfort, he becomes aware that the fragmentary moments of his earthly existence did not lead to happiness. When everything crumbles to dust, one searches for the absolute, the stable, and the unfailing only with great hesitation and with a certain sense of futility.

Life consists in experiencing that which, in essence, cannot be permanent. We search for a rational explanation of why even our great discoveries, joys, and expectations are only a prelude to their own extinction. Thus, we learn that eternity cannot be just a continuation of life as

. . . .

we know it now. It cannot and should not be understood in terms of duration, but in terms of quality, in terms of what crosses over from the human to the divine, from the temporal to the eternal.

If a man die, shall he live again? Yes and no.

No, insofar as the burdens of this life will no longer be, and insofar as our consciousness must be purged from temporality and mortality.

Yes, insofar as the essence of life cannot perish and cannot remain hidden forever.

Job's predicament consists in reducing life to existential experience and in trying to deduce from temporal events absolute principles. Everything can begin anew, and everything can be recreated. But, for the time being, not even God is in full control of Job's life. Why not let it run its course while Job probes into the perplexities of his lot? Only at the door of eternity will Job, as well as any of us, finally understand why our physical death must be the prelude to our everlasting life.

. . . .

MEDITATION 32

"God puts no trust in his holy ones, And the heavens are not clean in his sight." (Job 15:15)

Eliphaz rebukes Job for trying to justify himself before God, an endeavor no one should attempt. Job's claim to righteousness exceeds Eliphaz's conception of it. Why contend with God and not simply accept the limits imposed on us? Shouldn't Job play the hand he was dealt and not refute the advice of his friends? We are excluded from a knowledge of divine essence. Thus, there is no holiness God can trust on earth. In fact, there is none that he can trust in heaven. That which is not God himself is inferior to God and cannot partake of perfection. Did Eliphaz know this, or is he entering the realm of sophistry with Job?

Eliphaz resorts to a bold argument. Since the heavens are not clean and since God cannot trust even his holy ones, how can Job entertain the thought of reaching righteousness? Wisdom requires realism. Expecting the impossible can only augment the frustration of the human condition. If Eliphaz is right, why should God even concern himself with life on earth? Should he not invest his power in cleansing his own heaven?

When Christ urged his followers to be perfect as their heavenly father is perfect, he did not mean to elevate the human to the level of the divine, nor to reduce God to their limitations. Certainly, the closer Job comes to an intuition of God's majesty, the more he enters into moods of self-denial. Our humanity dictates the bounds of our relationship to God. Has Eliphaz acquired a saner view of God than Job?

. . . .

Perhaps there is nowhere Job can flee from evil, and perhaps Eliphaz has gotten hold of a truth he himself cannot fathom. Every generation has, in its own way, asked the same question: "What is man, what is woman?" And every generation has left behind answers that satisfy no one. We were told from the beginning of the story of Job that the heavenly council includes God's adversary, full of malice, full of power, full of persuasion. God's majesty fills the universe, but there is disturbing evidence of his absence from so much in human affairs. Eliphaz has already pointed out to Job that no knowledge is sufficient to allow us to argue with God. Job's quest appears arrogant, for it could not proceed without the assumption of a wisdom forbidden to mortals. Even the heavens are deprived of such an attainment. Job's journey was fated to end up in an impasse. Neither he nor his friends possess a map that would have shown a way out.

Eliphaz's response to Job sounds like a plea for realistic self-analysis. Job is not entitled to more wisdom than anybody else, and certainly not to a monopoly on it. His plight must be evaluated in the light of the common bond of humanity. Is there really anything new under the sun? How many Jobs have crossed existence without ever being noticed? Job's uniqueness resides primarily in his consciousness of what happens to him, a gift not very common in antiquity. He finds himself a stranger in his own world and has concluded that God has withdrawn from the scene, not an altogether erroneous conclusion.

How much does God intervene in human affairs? No one can answer such a question. Therefore, we must learn to be satisfied with the traditional views of God's providence. Eliphaz's argument seems quite convincing and could apply to the great majority of people. But God

. . . .

has now created a dilemma for Eliphaz to resolve. How is he to deal with the justice and righteousness of a faithful worshiper who refuses to stay within the traditional views of religion? And doesn't God take pride in the extraordinary virtue of Job, of one who can frustrate even Satan? Notwithstanding Eliphaz's argument, there must now be a place in God's heaven for those who cannot reach divine perfection, yet refuse the fate of being only human.

. . . .

MEDITATION 33.

"God has worn me out." (Job 16:7)

Not a fair contest! Did Job think that he could muster enough strength to contend with God? Does he not remember that Jacob could only limp after Peniel? In every encounter with God we lose part of our self, and, as in the case of Jacob, also part of our physical strength.

As time passes, it becomes evident to Job that he has become a servant of God to be wounded in his body and his soul. He is condemned to trudge across the desolate landscape of his exhausted world. Can anybody remain intact after encountering God?

In popular expectation, encountering God should bring blessings to life. Job, however, was forced to know better. One does not win against God; one learns humility. The presence of God in our midst exposes more clearly the dichotomy between the divine and the human. Nothing remains natural in such an encounter. What cannot mix does not provide a ground for either comfort or peace. Whatever the reasons for Job's dismay, he realizes that divine will does not systematically favor human expectation. This is why the Old Testament does not even attempt to reply to the logical question: Why do the evil prosper and why do the righteous suffer?

Job contemplates his predicament with anger, which he is tempted to attribute to God. But no such anthropomorphism can enlighten the situation. He has discovered

. . . .

that the qualities we attribute to God represent our conceptions of divinity. Fatigue and discouragement belong to specific human experiences. It is doubtful that God has worn Job out. Rather, Job has worn himself out trying to understand his plight in the light of divine action. Moral, spiritual, and intellectual inadequacies hinder our pursuit of ultimate knowledge. Job's distress resides in the awareness of his existential dilemma.

At times it must have appeared to Job that he was alone against the universe. Deprived of his children, sometimes rebuked by his wife, locked in endless and inconclusive arguments with his well-meaning friends, he searched for the anchors which might bring stability to his wavering thoughts. God could assign limits to the seas, decree the height of the mountains, and throw the stars across the firmament. But he would not, for a time at least, protect one of his servants from the agony of knowing himself in the midst of a reality in need of special compassion. Job had not yet heard the prophetic voice of the Messiah: "Come unto me, all who labor and are heavy laden, and I will give you rest."

In all generations, some of God's chosen people have to live in a divine "not yet." They are called upon to suffer in their bodies and souls the pains of the struggle of good versus evil. They die to their own comfort and peace so others can live. Often they do not know the results of their struggle. They offer to the world an unintentional sacrifice, sometimes never appreciated by others and sometimes venerated only generations after their death. Job only knows that he is worn out. The meaning will come later, beyond his personal awareness of it.

When one steps out of the traditional and the normal and dares to confront the divine, the outcome is rarely reassuring. Wisdom does not come from study or reflection. It is rooted in an analysis of what constitutes the truly human and the truly divine. In such a search, few find immediate relief. At this point Job sees only one side of the contest: his own. God remains hidden: *Deus absconditus*. The picture is incomplete and will remain so for a long time. Eternity alone will reveal what we cannot know now. Then only will there be true rest. In our earthly existence, we must be prepared to be worn out, not by God's design, but by virtue of our humanness.

. . . .

MEDITATION 34.

"O earth, cover not my blood, and let my cry find no resting place." (Job 16:18)

The intensity of suffering deserves a perpetual memorial. When earthly and heavenly powers conspire to destroy the innocent, some collective memory must become the repository of the anguish piercing through the empty spaces of infinity. The soul searches for its peace.

Job could no longer find the kind of atonement that would ease his injury and erase his scars. The day of death must express its power more than the frustrations of life. Peace must prevail through vindication. The troubled soul does not easily relinquish its hope in exchange for empty promises. The wager between God and his adversary has run its course, but Job pursues a quest beyond what the heavenly powers expected.

"O earth, cover not my blood." Job's destroyer should see his soul in its full unhappiness. Let the one who spills his blood also know that he does not wish eternal rest at the price of closing his eyes to undeserved affliction. The blood of the victim will always cry from the earth as a reminder of all the Cains of the world and as the plea for justice from all the Abels of creation. Only putting away the blood by burying the dead could finally resolve all antagonistic forces.

Both Greeks and Hebrews in antiquity subscribed to the idea that no soul can be at rest until the body receives proper burial. When Odysseus visits the realm of Hades, he is distraught at the torment of the soul of Elpenor whose

. . . .

body has not received a proper burial. Once out of Hades, Odysseus promptly fulfills the promise of a proper burial for Elpenor, whose spirit could finally find eternal rest. Similarly, Antigone accepts death to rescue her brother from a law forbidding his burial.

Ezekiel formulates the same conception for the Hebrews. After voicing an allegorical prophetic curse against Jerusalem and its people, he concludes: "Woe to the bloody city . . . for the blood she has shed is still in the midst of her; she put it on the bare rock, she did not pour it upon the ground to cover it with dust. To rouse my wrath, to take vengeance, I have set on the bare rock the blood she has shed, that it may not be covered."

Job feels moved to expose as the destroyer of his being the God he has worshiped his whole life. He wants to endow infinite suffering with an infinite voice of indignation and with a cry of defiance: "Let my cry find no resting place." For that he implores the earth not to cover his blood. He likens his plight to that of a condemned criminal who is denied burial so that his soul may suffer.

For now Job has abandoned the idea of winning God's favor. He knows that the divinity remains constantly jealous and interfering. He has learned from the sayings of Moses that God is a jealous God. But jealous of mortals? How could that fit into any universal and eternal scheme of creation and redemption? Yet Job is condemned to an absence of catharsis, to a tragic sense of life that can no longer be alleviated by ritual religion, to a moral conscience that cannot free itself from oppressive guilt, rightly or wrongly perceived. At one point, Job was the most successful and righteous person, and God could take credit for it. Now that he is the image of destitution, could God be blamed?

. . . .

"Even now, behold, my witness is in heaven." Does Job take God as a witness against God? Would this not be the apex of absurdity? Who is the witness in heaven against the God who strikes Job in his flesh and in his soul? Job has already learned and accepted that the same God can give and take away and still remain the God to be praised in all eternity. He can also be the God who destroys and redeems. Such a divine status and action may remain incomprehensible within our conceptual framework.

But all will be resolved when, in a few years, Job will have to leave everything behind and go the way from which he shall not return. In the perspective of that eternity, what will remain in the memory fed by the events and thoughts that kept Job riveted to earthly existence? Heavenbound is the soul, while the body returns to dust.

Once in the presence of his redeemer, will Job still pray that earth not cover his blood? With the soul finally at peace, will the cry of defiance still be necessary? Will God allow us to carry into eternity that which was so important to us while struggling with the vicissitudes of an earthly existence?

Death conveys a sense of finality. The fear of eternal oblivion appears even more unbearable than the prospect of nonbeing. It would seem that after years of suffering and turmoil one would welcome the peace of death, the serenity of eternal nothingness.

The request of Job is a plea to God not to forget the agony meted out to us by the forces of evil. The unhappy human memory must find its place within divine memory. At the moment, the only consolation Job can entertain is that his suffering can serve as a perpetual reminder of the pitfalls of life. God can no longer be proclaimed only as

. . . .

the dispenser of blessings. He is also the one involved in the struggle to bring his creation to redemption. The blood of the martyrs of all ages testifies to God's redemptive intent. Perhaps, in our own spiritual journey, we should not cover the blood or stifle the voice of God's suffering servants.

. . . .

MEDITATION 35.

"Since thou hast closed their minds to understanding."
(Job 17:4)

clectic God—what a strange concept! Our wisdom cannot be allowed to frustrate divine purpose. The Scriptures abound in sayings that reveal a carefully controlled use of human intelligence when it comes to the fulfillment of God's intentions. The heart of Pharaoh was hardened. Some prophets wondered why we possess qualities of knowledge just to be prevented from using them. Even Christ suggested that God's revelation may have to be hidden from the wise and the intelligent. Could the story of Job be understood outside of those divine modes of behavior?

Standing in the midst of a tempest that shattered his life, Job was in earnest need of support and comfort. But God put on his path friends and foes whose understanding was obscured. One can detect a tinge of malice in God's approach, and Job does not fail to complain. Even at the door of his grave, he cannot find solace, for God has allowed his mockers to have the upper hand. His friends are of no avail either. They could have served as a guarantee before God that Job was a righteous person. But how could anybody trust those who are no longer in full possession of their mental faculties?

Few biblical sayings have caused more grief to interpreters and exegetes than the affirmation we find in the prophet Isaiah and repeated by Christ. After his vision in the temple, the prophet is informed by God that those

. . . .

who have ears will not hear, those who have eyes will not see, and those who have minds will not understand. And all of this on the basis of a divine decision to keep people from discovering God's purpose: "Make the heart of these people fat, and their ears heavy, and shut their eyes; lest they see with their eyes, and hear with their ears, and understand with their hearts, and turn and be healed."

For Job the most absurd scenario would be the triumph of those without understanding. He entertains such a possibility. His journey to this point has taken place on roads full of obstacles and injuries. Nothing can reassure him any more that there is a divine design which conforms to his expectations. He has to pursue mysteries he is not willing to acknowledge.

All understanding comes from God. He reserves the right to reveal or not to reveal the details of his relationship to Job or to anyone else. The chaos of the world cannot be dispelled by the effort of the intellect. Were it so, God might become unnecessary. Our knowledge depends on divine illumination, in which case it is granted to us as a gift and not on the basis of our achievements.

The mockers who deride Job are made, not born. We are all equal at birth, and we are all equal in death, bringing nothing into life and taking nothing with us at the end. In between we grope to grasp the mysteries of a world eluding our categories of knowledge.

Job finds comfort in the conviction that God reserves the right to withhold from his opponents the power of understanding. Perpetual injustice would become unbearable. The triumph of it could mean endless indignation. Those who would have the power to transform absurdities into eternal verities must be deprived of such

. . . .

a possibility. Chaos could not be God's purpose for his creation. Consequently, understanding is meted out only where it supports the right kind of purpose. Could Job be right? Certainly not! The godless, at times, do possess a lot of understanding. And it happens many times that those who claim to be God's servants reveal disturbing levels of mediocrity.

Job does not wish to be subjected to perspectives on life that would mock of his experience. In certain cases it is preposterous to try to explain God's actions. The fear of knowing is as great as the curse of ignorance. Without admitting it, Job prefers his plight to the knowledge of friends or foes whose understanding is unrelated to divine illumination. But then again, if God has the power to withhold understanding from Job's friends, could he not also treat Job in the same manner?

MEDITATION 36.

"If I look for Sheol as my house, . . . where then is my hope?" (Job 17:13–15)

depleted soul, tired of the noises of the world, would seek in the wilderness the solitude that could bring comfort. In the same way Job has entertained the thought of descending to the Sheol of nothingness in order to escape the unbearable pursuit of God. Death might provide the final separation, the absence of consciousness, and the end of his tragedy.

To experience the peace of Sheol one must abandon all hope, for such a peace would require that one no longer be remembered by God. Yet it is God who apportions death, and his authority does not end with the physical annihilation of his children.

Job scrupulously performs all the rites expected by his God. When stricken in body and soul he continues to praise the wisdom of the creator. When in a state of rebellion, he blames his own inadequacy. When confronting a God he can no longer understand, he argues with sagacity and passion. When his friends give him advice, he listens but does not follow it, for he feels it to be void of compassion and relevance. When his wife pleads with him, he exposes the foolishness of her reasoning. When he finds himself alone in the throes of affliction, he musters courage to pursue a quest that leads nowhere but to annihilation of hope and faith. Now at the end of a journey whose different moments never formed a coherent picture, he allows himself to conceive of a dreamless existence in the shadowy realm of Sheol.

. . . .

From anguished solitude to the wish of nothingness the road can be very short. That which frightens the multitude fills Job with a new expectation, with a kind of negative salvation totally absent of any desire to remain connected with God. He knows of the prophetic voice which has warned the living that in Sheol memory will be so limited as to forbid any notion of complete life and that there will be no proclamation or praise of God. "In Sheol who can give thee praise," exclaims the Psalmist. To that the prophet Isaiah adds: "For Sheol cannot thank thee, and death cannot praise thee. Those who go down to the pit cannot hope for thy faithfulness."

Job must acknowledge "Sheol is naked before God." But there is one advantage in the realm of the dead. With all possibility of proclamation and praise withdrawn, no one has to be concerned with or suffer the results of rewards or punishments. Thus, we find Job momentarily agreeable to the thought of absolute neutrality, a thought that gives him the hope of peace. But not for long. Absence of hope destroys life. Because hope must persist, Sheol loses its quality of neutrality and fills the soul of the dead with sorrow and visions of redemption.

Job's insight into the existence of Sheol betrays the same uneasiness other Old Testament writers share. The realm of the dead is also the place of oblivion and separation from God. But nothing in creation can escape the omnipresence of the creator. Job can no longer be certain that the God he could not escape in life will not pursue him in Sheol. He may have shared the Psalmist's idea of divine universality: "If I ascend to heaven, thou art there! If I make my bed in Sheol, thou art there!"

Perhaps the experience of nothingness is a necessary step toward a fuller appreciation of life, however marked

. . . .

by sorrow or joy. Out of the depth of nothingness come the cries of those who await redemption and who know that the Lord of creation will not forget them and that he will carry them out of their slumber in the realm of the shades. God cannot leave his servants in Sheol, for the purpose of creation is life, not death.

For a moment Job had forgotten that Sheol stands in opposition to God. As time went on, to quote the prophet Isaiah, "Sheol has enlarged its appetite and opened its mouth beyond measure." Job knew that Sheol reduces every power to weakness and that it depletes all of its indwellers of whatever greatness God put in them. Redemption rests partly on the hope that God cannot allow the gifts he placed in his creatures to be wasted or annihilated in Sheol. Those who welcome descent into Sheol simply fail to recognize the final purpose of creation.

We often have to make our peace with life, with whatever comes our way. And sometimes we meet those who contemplate in death the liberation from the burdens of temporality. In times of trouble some may seek the favors of the gods ruling the underworld so that they may be received there under good auspices. The prophet Isaiah arose against such practices by some rulers in the very city of God, Jerusalem. They dared proclaim, "We have made a covenant with death, and with Sheol we have an agreement; when the overwhelming scourge passes through it will not come to us." God ordered Isaiah to deny such arrangements and to predict ruin for those who enter them.

The God who rules over all and sees all keeps everyone in his eternal memory. He will recall all his own from Sheol when the right time arrives. But this does not comfort Job, as he sees in his journey to Sheol an irreversible

. . . .

finality: "As the cloud fades and vanishes, so he who goes down to Sheol does not come up; he returns no more to his house, nor does his place know him any more."

Later the Talmud attempts to dispel the notion that the soul might find refuge in Sheol: "Let not your impulse give you reassurances that the netherworld will prove a refuge to you—for against your will you were formed, against your will you were born, against your will you now live, against your will you will die, and against your will you will have to give account and reckoning before the king of kings, the holy one."

In his state of exhaustion and discouragement, how could Job save himself from rebellion? He has come to a tragic point at which no choice could be made. Life under his current circumstances compels him to wish for death. But the thought of death fills him with sorrow as he realizes that his whole being—his faith, his hope, and his striving through incredible suffering and doubt—may have all been in vain. So he offers to God the most unusual prayer; "Oh that thou wouldest hide me in Sheol, that thou wouldest conceal me until thy wrath be past, that thou wouldest appoint me a set time, and remember me!"

Perhaps it is within this strange dialectic of being forgotten and being remembered that Job could finally hope to find peace of heart and peace of mind. He may as well have prayed, "Forget me, O God, when your hand is ready to dispense evil and sorrow, and remember me when in your grace you can offer me compassion and salvation."

. . . .

MEDITATION 37.

"How long will you hunt for words?" (Job 18:2)

ere it possible for us to connect every situation and every thought with the right word, our small worlds might no longer appear chaotic. Bildad shows a great deal of frustration because the lines of communication between Job and his friends suffer from the scarcity of proper words to describe the experience of all involved.

Through simple and complex situations, we hunt for words to express our knowledge and feelings. While entertaining guests in our home in France, I was once confronted with a question that seemed simple enough. One of our guests who was not familiar with the multitude of cheeses available in French stores asked about the differences between them. What appeared at first as an easy task soon became an exercise in hunting for words. I finally suggested that the best way to know the difference between cheeses was to taste them.

On occasion we are not able to link the proper words to our experience. There is so much more to what we know and feel than what we can say. When we fail to find the right words to convey something of importance, we beg our listeners to penetrate our thoughts beyond the help we can provide through speech. We resort to expressions such as: "You know what I mean." How could anybody know what we mean if we are unable to verbalize it?

Hunting for words! In spite of his good intentions and genuine concern for Job, Bildad cannot mask

. . . .

his impatience. Long had Job and his friends tried to communicate and read each other's souls—in vain, for all stayed in the realm of superficiality. "Should we all partake of the same fate and stupidity as cattle?" cried Bildad. Certainly Job could have invested more reflection into his remarks and could have spoken of his situation more cogently. Who has not felt discouraged by the inability to communicate what deeply affects us? Many aspects of our personal essence can never be described for lack of proper words.

Language is power indeed, and poets and writers have constantly astonished us by putting at our disposal the conceptual framework necessary to undertake the journey into our inner selves. Yet, even their words are insufficient to open up the mysteries hidden within God's creation.

Job's plight could be understood and communicated in everyday language, but the hope he entertained and the mystery he sought to penetrate lay outside of the province of accessible words. Faith must invent its own language on a personal level. Even within our rational categories of thought, words can become irrelevant. Job's friends were caught up in an attempt to explain his situation within the context of traditional experience. Job himself failed to communicate to them his deep feelings. In the absence of a language common to all, no agreement could be reached on either human or divine intentions.

Some things should remain unsaid. Forcing words on situations may lead to the loss of a mystery God intends to keep. We were not meant to know everything, much less to explain all events. Wisdom requires that our words be few so we do not incur the risk of reducing the noble and the eternal to the absurd and the meaningless. The ability to accept that which is beyond our intellect is a major part of religion. Should we have the possibility to grasp and explain everything, God would lose his mysterious transcendence.

The reproach of Bildad may have been sincere and correct. Why hunt for words if we surmise that they might not be the proper representatives of our emotions and fears, as well as of our hopes and expectations? Hunting for words will remain one of our major activities, for we cannot surrender to ignorance and uncertainty. When faith fails to provide an entry into God's mysteries, our intellect strives to know what may remain forbidden to us. Thus, to the creation of words there will be no end.

. . . .

MEDITATION 38.

"Know then that God has put me in the wrong, and closed his net about me." (Job 19:6)

he unreality of reality! How useless to analyze a world God places out of our reach. Job must continue on a journey he did not devise and accept the will of a God who has retreated beyond his grasp. His surroundings have become unreal, his friends exasperating. The world he knew and the stage on which he now plays out his life have lost all points of contact. All truly human feelings are forbidden to him because he no longer lives in a human world. Like a puppet in the market place, his movements and his thoughts are directed by a master who no longer allows self-determination. Job cries out that God has deprived him of hope, expectation, and equanimity.

When we err, we must pay the price. When God chooses to do what appears wrong to us, our lives are disrupted. Why then do Job's friends criticize his indignation? Job's alienation from both friends and God leaves him in the most poignant of all existential situations. He must create his own freedom to experience whatever he chooses to experience. But he must also accept his anxiety when he realizes that he has to face life alone, without divine help or favor. In those specific circumstances neither God nor friends can be of any help to him. Divine support is not our automatic due and may not be extended to us until the net is closed about us. Job found no cause for rejoicing in that situation, unlike what Père Teilhard de Chardin expressed more recently: "Lord, what is there in suffering that commits me so deeply to you? Why should

. . . .

my wings flutter more joyfully than before when you stretch out nets to imprison me?"

If it is correct that religion is what we do with our solitariness, then the greatest of all religious figures must be Job. Normally solitariness is a choice. In this case, it is imposed on Job by a God who withdraws his support. If God must strike, stricken indeed Job will remain. And in all of this he wonders about the reality of life and the meaning of divine fair play. The loss of his material goods was not, after all, extremely important. All could be replaced. But the loss of his children struck him deeply. The events that followed left him a diminished person feeling that so much of what he was will never be retrieved.

Job's heartbreak comes from the fact that in all of his tribulations he still knows of God. When Satan took everything away from him, God did not allow the obliteration of Job's consciousness of the divine. Thus, Job is condemned to believe in a God who, in his eternal inviolability, need not concern himself with aberrations that render human life meaningless. Divine wrath never returns to God unfulfilled; it engenders within the heart of the victims a yearning for eternal justice and vindication.

Trapped within a sense of divine abandonment, or worse, divine malice, Job begins to travel the dangerous road which leads from indignation to the temptation of cursing the universe and its maker. Having come face to face with an enduring reality of meaningless fragments, Job succumbs to the temptation of viewing the entire creation from his personal vantage point. The search for the stable and unfailing remains futile when the heart is downcast and in the powerful grips of discouragement.

Job found it difficult to accept that God is always more than what we know and believe. Sometimes we have

. . . .

to seek his presence in an alien and hostile environment that appears intent on destroying our equanimity. The scars of misfortune persist longer than the words of comfort. Job wants his friends to know that he is in contention with God and that he is losing the battle. Faith can be expressed in rebellion as much as in servile obedience. Such a proposition might even serve as a summary for the Book of Job.

If to know God is to suffer, and if to suffer is to know God, then Job must learn that the path which leads from time to eternity renders the reality of life unreal. For only in the devastation of the material world and human physical reality can the realm of spirituality be born. But why has God chosen to create a world we must escape in order to find him? "Behold I cry out 'violence!' but I am not answered; I call aloud, and there is no justice!" is for the moment Job's painful realization that God may choose silence and distance in order to reveal to us what it means to be alone with our inner self.

MEDITATION 39.

"I know that my Redeemer lives." (Job 19:25)

ry of hope or cry of despair? At last Job knows that there must be in eternity's eons a vindicator who can be swayed neither by divine whim nor by evil malice. Vindication rescues life from absurdity. Suffering that does not create its redemption remains cruel and inhumane. Beyond Job's destitution there must emerge the ultimate vindicator who reintroduces a sense of reality into a world of senseless experience. Plato urged his students to strive to become like the divinity. For Job, the divinity must be forced into human experience. God must come to know us in all our humanity. The creator can never be released from his obligation toward his creation.

At last a vindicator will stand on the very dust that covers Job's sores. Justice will prevail because goodness must triumph. All this happens in a realm of unreality not to be seen, not to be heard, and not to be known except in the depths of solitude.

Job is now alone, far from his friends who could not penetrate a realm Satan can no longer destroy and God alone can illuminate. For the time being the vindicator is faceless, the product of Job's yearning.

The barrier which stood between Job and God must come down, however visible or invisible. He was hoping to be restored to strength and to live the rest of his life with intensity and dignity, but he could no longer get there on his own. Somewhere God's compassion must

. . . .

be stored for times of need. But who could bring it down to the sufferer, to the victim of forces unleashed in a creation out of control?

Job knows that a vindicator will appear. Mercy supersedes justice, but Job needs both. His heart does not dare hope. His mind is lost in thoughts deprived of cogency. It is no longer Job alone, but the whole earth crying out for salvation. Creation will yearn for its redemption to the last day of its existence, until it becomes a new creation. In the midst of it, we keep searching for vindicators who might renew our hope and faith.

The divine hand touched Job much too often for him not to believe that God's pursuit of him must stop. But it cannot be stopped by Job himself. It is time for a redeeming presence to interpose itself between Job's powerlessness and God's supremacy. A redeemer, or vindicator, must share both the divine and the human sides of life. Were it not so, death would annihilate the human side, leaving neither God nor his children fulfilled in any creative purpose. To stand on our side, the redeemer must oppose, or at least control, any divine necessity of retribution.

There is a part of our destiny that is sealed in God's heaven. And there is part of our destiny that is not irrevocably fixed, a destiny we can accept or we can rebel against, a destiny we can influence by the power of the will, a destiny that could be altered by circumstances of our making. But in a state of exhaustion, we may forfeit our privileges of free will.

Beyond all adversity there is God. But Job feels that within adversity we may become unable to keep a close contact with our creator. At last beyond failure, doubt, and absurdity, a vindicator will stand upon the earth and turn all suffering into a new revelation. When that comes, what will the heart feel and the mind know? Was Thoreau right in suggesting that "not till we are lost do we begin to understand ourselves?"

For the time being Job's redeemer is a cry of faith, a wish that his misery be written in a book or inscribed on a rock, so even God might come to notice it: "Oh that my words were written! Oh that they were inscribed in a book! Oh that with an iron pen and lead they were graven in the rock for ever!"

The words of Job have now echoed throughout eternity, having become real in the person of Christ through whom the Jobs of all times can have an audience with God. Who else but Job could proclaim that human frailty need not succumb to despair and self-annihilation?

MEDITATION 40.

"Why do the wicked live, reach old age, and grow mighty in power?" (Job 21:7)

hen bad things happen to good people, we are prone to entertain the notion that divine justice is betrayed. When good things happen to bad people, we are puzzled by unfairness. God's creation does not exhibit any fundamental principle of justice. It does not verify the theoretical proposition that good is rewarded and evil punished.

The Talmud quotes Rabbi Yannai as saying, "Within our reach is neither the tranquility of the wicked nor even the suffering of the righteous." To that two comments are offered. The first one reads, "At the tranquility of the wicked we have not arrived, the sufferings of the righteous we have not approached." The second tries to give an interpretation: "It is not within our power to understand why the way of the wicked prospers and why the righteous are made to endure sufferings. But it seems to me the saying means this . . . we do not enjoy the kind of tranquility the wicked enjoy . . . and the sufferings we endure are not like those of the righteous, but are sufferings meted out as a punishment."

Zophar tries to convince Job that there exists a divine norm of retribution according to which evil is short-lived. But Job knows from experience no such standard of justice exists. What then should one's relationship to God be? Any reflection in that area only accentuates our discouragement in a world so little in tune with our moral aspirations. "The greatest cause of sadness," proposes

. . . .

Boethius, "resides in the fact that in spite of a good helmsman to guide the world evil can still exist and go unpunished. That this can happen in the realm of an omniscient and omnipotent God who wills only good is beyond perplexity and complaint."

Job's plight fails to illuminate his friends' conception of the existence of evil. They have adopted a rational stance; according to it, there exists a logical way to deal with human aberrations. From a purely religious viewpoint, they are right. Virtue must be rewarded and evil chastised. But by whose criteria does one determine right and wrong? And why does God refrain from intervening in human affairs for such long periods of time?

In a broken creation, why doesn't God mend the pieces and restore well-being? Plutarch wrote an entire volume trying to answer the puzzling question of why there is so much delay in divine vengeance against the wicked, a question that cannot be answered to everybody's satisfaction. It always depends on how we choose to interpret it. Plutarch chose the following explanation for the delay of God's vengeance: "We should become cautious in such matters, and hold the gentleness and magnanimity displayed by God a part of virtue that is divine, which by punishment amends a few, while it profits and admonishes many by the delay."

Job protects himself by offering a lengthy discourse explaining his frustration. Contrary to every hope that had sustained his faith, he allowed himself to be overcome by the feeling that religion is useless and prayer unprofitable. God refuses to comply with the principles we try to impose on him. The existence of evil does not affect his essence. It matters only to us, as we connect divine creative power with a strong sense of ultimate perfection.

. . . .

At points we may feel that God violates his own principles according to which creation should function. The separation of good and evil is neither possible nor desirable on the level we would like it to happen. Didn't Christ suggest that we should let the weeds grow with the grain until the harvest, so we do not destroy the good with the evil? Caught in a web of ever-changing circumstances, we are deprived of satisfactory insights into divine providence and human fate.

We err when we believe that evil affects divine being. It must be removed not because of God but because of us. Our perplexity often originates in our ignorance. It is because we fail to comprehend the divine purpose of what surrounds us that we may be led to believe that the wicked prosper and can achieve happiness.

That which is external to God happens to be profoundly important for us. Job finds this unbearable. He can accept neither the seemingly rational argument of his friends, nor the idea that God should be indifferent to injustice. What would the world look like if our notion of justice triumphed? We do have a strong sense of justice. Why doesn't God comply with it? For the time being, Job is learning the hard way that we cannot secure God's blessing through our own sense of righteousness. How then are we to achieve it?

Job pleads for nothing less than the vindication of goodness. God's governance cannot hinge on the temporary success of those undeserving. Divine creation must in the end reflect perfection or stop being viewed as divine creation. As we travel through the Book of Job and survey the landscape of human events, we marvel at the ability of some of us to pursue goodness as the highest virtue achievable.

. . . .

In the end, neither the heart nor the mind allow absolute resignation. The will to prevail over tribulations compels us to seek within ourselves peace, strength, and determination. No amount of evidence in favor of the existence of evil has been able to deprive us of the belief in ultimate goodness. In his acceptance speech for the Nobel Prize, William Faulkner reflected on the atmosphere of fear which pervaded a shaken society. He chose to emphasize the ability of the human spirit to create out of the materials of discouragement something which did not exist before. He concluded, "I decline to accept the end of man. . . . I believe that man will not only endure: he will prevail."

For those who, like Job, encounter life realistically, the belief in goodness cannot perish. It is the only persuasive force that helps us ride out of the night of uncertainty stronger and with a deeper sense of the noble and spiritual within us. In moments of tragedy we respond with a great amount of magnanimity stored within us, sometimes beyond our knowledge of our own resources.

True, not everybody seeks the good, and not everybody finds it. But the good has no reality apart from its presence in us, whatever poor receptacles we may be for it. Thus, any discourse on life must sooner or later lead to a reflection on the basic worth which makes it possible. This is what brought Job to the limits of credibility. In the greatest moments of rebellion, his protest is determined by his unwavering faith that in the end he will know the purpose of God.

The mystery of goodness is that we remain capable of believing in it and of practicing it even when everything conspires to prove to us that it has withdrawn from

. . . .

the human scene. Those who have read the book or seen the film *Schindler's List* may still wonder why and how so much concern and help could have come out of an individual in spite of himself. From all points of view, Oskar Schindler was an unlikely hero. There was something more than himself in what he was doing.

In the realm of faith, goodness posits itself as one of the major links capable of connecting us to God. In this world, we shall continue to seek the signposts pointing to the realization of our essence and creative purpose. Like Job, we may be dismayed that the wicked prosper and achieve power. But we must learn how to understand our participation in the tragic side of life.

Are there many more bets in heaven between God and Satan than that of Job's case? Every day we may raise our voices in indignation when we see evil triumph. But at the same time we should ask the question: What does it mean in the perspective of divine eternity?

MEDITATION 41.

"Agree with God, and be at peace." (Job 22:21)

The Roman stoic philosopher Seneca wrote a treatise on divine providence at a time when he was faced with turbulent events that would eventually cost him his life. He wanted to share with his friends his belief that "God hardens, reviews, and disciplines those whom he approves, whom he loves." Later he wrote an epistle in the form of a reflection on his moral journey. In it we find the following statement: "When everything seems to go hard and uphill, I have trained myself not merely to obey God, but to agree with His decisions. I follow Him because my soul wills it, and not because I must. Nothing will ever happen to me that I shall receive with ill humour or with a wry face."

The advice of Eliphaz to Job sounds very similar: "Agree with God, and be at peace." The argument rests on the logical assumption that nothing human could be profitable to God and that in his contention with his creator Job will be the loser. Since he is at a definite disadvantage, it would be better for him to submit to what appears to be God's will.

But submission and subservience cannot lay the proper foundation for the religion of a person whose integrity does not allow him to have recourse to expedient solutions. If God is to possess Job's heart, he must earn his respect and loyalty and not demand it through force. Job wants to be at peace, but he cannot for the time being agree with God.

. . . .

Agreement implies mutual understanding, a phenomenon neither God nor Job enjoy so far. Job refuses to step into a religion that would deprive him of his essence. Suffering may preclude peace, but renunciation would destroy faith. Eliphaz's perspective appears irrefutable, mostly when one considers the frailty of our historical situations and the precariousness of human judgments. Job, however, protests his fate of being at the mercy of destructive forces.

Religious tenets end up betraying their source. Job's friends feel comfortable with their views of God, but God chose to break the pattern in order to ascertain the endurance and loyalty of Job. There is much to gain, says Eliphaz, by submitting to God. But Job is not interested in the beneficial side of religion. He would rather compel God to reveal the reasons for his actions. There must be mutual respect in any relationship with God. Eliphaz would not dare venture into such a religious stance.

To be at peace does not automatically signify that we live in communion with God. God's presence keeps us uneasy and unsettled. In Job's case, the principle operates beyond the possibility of peace. Therefore, Job has to muster much more than the usual ways of dealing with religious issues.

If God desires a broken and humble heart, he got only part of that in Job, who is not totally impressed by the need for humility. Know he must, and know he will. Peace, however, will remain out of reach. In all of this, Job keeps his righteousness and does not offend God.

To live at peace has remained an unachievable dream for Job's race. Wars, droughts, idolatry, and calamities

. . . .

of all kinds have forced the Hebrew nation to postpone any realization of peace until the advent of the messianic era. Shalom remained an eschatological hope. Some day everything will be at peace, entire and complete in the eyes of God and his people. But for now, peace is hidden, though all things in God's creation are linked together by the power of the Father of all. In our temporal situation, we surmise the unity and harmony of all things. But it is not given to us to know why. As the poet Francis Thompson says, "Thou canst not stir a flower without troubling a star."

When circumstances keep our heart in turmoil, only faith can open the door of eternity. Job has learned how to live concurrently in two different realities: existential anguish and faith. It does not always bring reassurance to him. Too many mysteries of life remain beyond human knowledge. Yet, faith has to be the only recourse.

"Agree with God." Sincere advice, but how difficult! It requires either the simplistic approach of Eliphaz or the frightening search in which Job finds himself against his will. Faith would require that we not question God, that we assume him continuously right and benevolent. Job has opted for a different route leading to a knowledge of God's intentions. In the process, he may have to forfeit peace and face with courage the liabilities of his daring. Still worse, he may not find it possible to agree with God until he discerns the proper reasons to do so. His suffering has taught him that revolt and rebellion do not systematically take us away from God.

The most dangerous situation is to have a little faith, that is a faith which is never tested in the tragedies of life. Eliphaz's advice resembles the kind we could receive in popular belief. Job ventures out of that realm. Unbeknownst to him, he finds himself in what Saint Paul later defines as a fight against the principalities and powers which are in heaven.

Eliphaz is not ready to concede that agreeing with God does not always bring peace. It may throw us into turmoil. Moses encountered God in the burning bush only to enter into a lifetime of struggle, constantly contending with both God and his people. The bush remained burning in the life of Job. It is still burning for those who dare approach it and know that encounter with God may bring more conflict than peace in our quest for salvation.

MEDITATION 42.

"Oh, that I knew where I might find him!" (Job 23:3)

D*eus absconditus!* God the remote and the inaccessible, choosing silence when we need most to hear his word!

While the Babylonian armies invaded Judah, the Jewish leaders begged Jeremiah to consult God. People were fleeing in droves to Egypt. The situation was desperate. Yet God waited ten days before he replied to Jeremiah. Does God share our sense of urgency? Where is God when we need him most? Jeremiah knew the strange feeling of God's distance. The closer we come to him, the more remote he appears to us. Isaiah summarized it thus: "Truly, thou art a God who hidest thyself, O God of Israel, the Savior." Yet hope must prevail: "I will wait for the LORD, who is hiding his face from the house of Jacob, and I will hope in him."

Job surmises what led Pascal to exclaim, "The eternal silence of those infinite spaces frightens me." He is terrified by the one-sided contest. If only God would agree to a debate! There, in a reasonable and fair exchange, Job knows he would be delivered from his misfortune.

Why then does God hide himself? Does God find himself uneasy with Job's argument? There is no sense of fair play when God can destroy at will from a distance but never comes close enough for a serious debate.

Who might be the one who will now prevail in an agon that pits against each other two unevenly matched protagonists? The contest has already lasted for

. . . .

too long. Too many questions have been raised, and too many debates have taken place. Divine patience and human determination fail to find a common ground. Job begins to entertain the notion of a dark side of God. In a world full of threatening forces, divine intervention might provide immediate relief. Why doesn't it happen? Who shall ever understand why Satan must have his chance at experimenting with the human race?

In a *tête-à-tête* argument, Job might have the better chance. This, however, assumes an orderly creation. But the world of Job does not reflect perfection. God never manifests himself in an obvious fashion. We have to force our way into divine mysteries. Redemption cannot rest on logic and reasoning but on a radically altered concept of creative power. Only in a contest with the forces of evil could Job discover the compassionate side of God.

Job concludes that he labors in vain, for without finding God he cannot verify the validity of his arguments. They all sound good to him, but how would God respond to them? For the time being, the distance between God and Job has become unbearable. Reading God's mind at such a distance cannot yield either hope or well-being. The dialectic of hope and fear, though strange, remains the only plausible alternative.

Hope of seeing God often turns to awe when we become aware of the gap which keeps him away from us. The only reassurance is that God cannot err in the ends he assigns. The stars fail to shine when hidden by dark clouds, some being eternal, others representing our passing somber moods. The worst might be to stop at the gateway of the wasteland and conclude that God is indifferent to our determination to seek communion with him. "Only that day dawns to which we are awake," proposes

. . . .

Thoreau. Sometimes it seems that our function in life resides in recovering what has always been there, even if it is unknown to us.

"Oh, that I knew where I might find him!" There are not many places that have escaped the scrutiny of Job. He has looked everywhere within God's creation. He has contemplated everything that could have mirrored God's presence. Nothing truly reflects his anguish and his dread. As he continues the journey, hoping to stumble on some proofs of his righteousness, he finds only the inaccessible and the mysterious. And his soul begins to ache, even more than before.

. . . .

MEDITATION 43.

"I am terrified at his presence." (Job 23:15)

f the fear of the Lord is the beginning of wisdom, for Job it may have been the end of what he was willing to learn. Hemmed in by darkness, faint in heart, and overwhelmed by a destiny God alone assigns and fulfills to the end, Job resigned himself to live in the presence of heavenly decrees which stirred nothing but dread in his spiritual outlook. He has now learned the greatest lesson of all time: a God we could comprehend would cease to be God.

Those who dare question God have to learn that the Lord of creation never discloses himself in any final way. God remains beyond everything we know, feel, say, hope, and pray for. To yearn for God is to accept the mystery of the unattainable, for God can never be reduced to the grasp of our intellectual and mental faculties. In our mystical union with the divine, we must come to face the "wholly other," that which at times produces in our hearts awe and fascination, and at other times fear and apprehension.

The "wholly other!" The holy presence which does not correspond to anything germane to our experience cannot fill us with joy. It is only when our spiritual eyes perceive the sacred nature of God that we enter his temple with fear and trembling and, like Isaiah, sing: "Holy, holy, holy is the LORD of hosts; the whole earth is full of his glory." And not until the seraphim touches our lips with the burning coal are we capable of entering into communion with our maker.

. . . .

Job did not have his seraphim. For a time he stood on the other side of the great divide, wishing for peace while terrified by the power of a God impervious to his love or to his rebellion. His experience became personal. One does not survive meeting God face to face. This is perhaps where traditional religion comes to our rescue. When we reduce God to rituals and to platitudes, we need no longer be concerned with his terrifying presence and need no longer enter his temple with fear and trembling. Job would have spared himself a great deal of misfortune by accepting the sophistry of his friends.

Gone were the days when Job could perform his prescribed rituals and feel confident that he had satisfied divine requirements. He learned at the cost of ineffable tragedies that the closer we come to God, the farther removed in his mystery he appears to us. He knew the futility of his wish to elucidate divine inscrutability. Like Job we feel lost in God's fatherly arms, not because we do not belong there, but because they are too vast to contain us in our insignificance.

But why the dread of God and the feeling of terror in his presence? Is it because of the majesty of God, or is it also because we come to know ourselves in our true position in the cosmos? Fear comes from a lack of understanding. Job could no longer fathom the will of God. But did he have the right insight into his own person?

There is a part of our spiritual being that transcends our perception of it, something which belongs to the intuition of the divine in us but which cannot always be communicated in words. As Teilhard de Chardin puts it, "It is through that which is most incommunicably personal that we make contact with the universal." Alone in the immensity of God's universe, misunderstood by

. . . .

everybody, Job could reflect on his own terror without being able to share it with anyone, for there was none who truly journeyed with him through the desolation of his suffering. Plotinus remarks, "The divine is not expressible, so the initiate is forbidden to speak of it to anyone who has not been fortunate enough to have beheld it himself."

What is it indeed that Job beheld that made him the most fortunate of unfortunate servants of God? Whatever it was, it could not be comprehended by others then, nor since. The story of Job is not about Job, but about every person who appears in this world and seeks to discover within himself or herself the divine gifts that go unnoticed until in solitude, in humility, and in fear, we stand in the presence of a God whose eternity we could not fathom while we were seduced by temporal aspirations.

Even more than Job, Chrysostom exposed the arrogance of those who lay claim to a knowledge of God: "It is an impertinence to say that He who is beyond the apprehension of even the higher Powers can be comprehended by us earthworms, or compassed and comprised by the weak forces of our understanding!" To great mystics, God remains inexpressible. They know that drawing nearer to God only fills us with awe and, as in the case of Job, with terror. When we try to express the ineffable, we discover that there are no words in existence to convey our experience. There is a realm of divine communion that belongs to the inner *logos*, to the depths of being we cannot share with others.

The greatness of God produces our solitude.

Though God was the God of the whole people, there was in fact in Israel no collective understanding of

. . . .

him. Instead there were the intuitions of the great personalities of the Old Testament: Abraham, Moses, Isaiah, Jeremiah, and so many others. In Job we reach the apex of the mysterious terror which overcomes the person who seeks divine presence.

At some point, we must stop our journey with Job and undertake our own. In the experience of Job we find the multiple pieces of our own search. Our quest must become personal, until we, too, come to realize that the religious world can provide only limited comfort. The discovery of God comes at the cost of great turmoil and suffering and cannot be but deeply personal.

As in the case of Job, our spiritual journey may lead us to a burning desire to be united with what at first was a source of terror. We cannot penetrate the greatest of all mysteries, namely that the ineffable God of eternity can live in the hearts of his children. Nor can we consider him absent from the tragedies and misfortunes that come our way. Job's rebellion turns to resignation: "For God will complete what he appoints for me." Or could we call Job's attitude faith? He knew that trust in God is not free from anguish. Once we commit our existential ship to the winds of eternity, we must sail where they blow; we forfeit our illusory privilege of assigning it a fixed destination. Momentarily Job allows his thoughts to scatter over the vast ocean of storms and fears, terrified by the immensity of the unknown, but reassured that God remains at the helm of his battered vessel.

Even in the grip of a terror rooted in our ignorance of God's design for our lives, we can resolve to hear the message every time we have to hear it. Terror has no absolute place within God's eternity. Yet God's eternity would be empty without it, for it could not contain us apart from our consciousness of his terrifying presence.

. . . .

MEDITATION 44.

"God pays no attention to their prayer." (Job 24:12)

e Profundis! When the souls of the wounded cry for help in the city of the dying, God refuses to hear. Why? Is Job beginning to entertain the concept of the powerlessness of God in the face of human sufferings? He remembers the times when his troubled people journeyed through spiritual desolation and through tragedies without any visible support from their God. When God remains silent and distant and when the people are like sheep without a shepherd, discouragement replaces faith.

At this point in life, Job puts forth a claim of obedience to God few of us could match: "I have not departed from the commandment of his lips; I have treasured in my bosom the words of his mouth." But he also realizes that God is unchangeable. God will fulfill Job's desires according to God's own will, and not according to Job's request.

What then is the value of prayer, since God can choose not to listen? The assumption that God should be there for us in time of need is a religious postulate that has guided his people forever. But Job also knows that we may have to accept God's distance, even when it troubles us: "Behold, I go forward, but he is not there; and backward, but I cannot perceive him; on the left hand I seek him, but I cannot behold him; I turn to the right hand, but I cannot see him. But he knows the way that I take."

. . . .

Who shall ever know whether the requests we present to God are according to his purpose and for our good? Could it be that God's providence manifests itself in his denial of requests which could harm us? If God answered every one of our prayers and wishes we may come to sorrow when we discover how ignorant we were of his design for our lives. We may want to heed the advice of learning how to pray before we present our petitions to God.

But how much of this applies to Job? Origen suggests that our life should be a continuous prayer and that prayer should be the highlight of our lives. Job belongs to the category of people Origen had in mind. Yet even Job found himself a participant in the suffering of those who inhabit the city of the dying. He has joined the cry for help of the souls of the wounded, and he too has concluded that God pays no attention to their prayers. How could he really know?

Can we infer from our misery that God is insensitive to our tragedies and catastrophes? God is not absent from our wars, famines, plagues, cruelties, and natural disasters. Nor do we need to entertain the notion of a powerless God. Like Job, we may bemoan the fact that our attempts at righteousness do not impress God. There are no standards by which we can evaluate God's purpose for his creation.

A little knowledge is dangerous. A great deal of knowledge leads to faith, not certainty. Those who have found absolute security in their religion may have moved away from God. When our spiritual eyes allow us an insight into God's majesty, the result is not certainty but unsettled hearts and minds. The suggestion of Erich Fromm that the search for certainty destroys the meaning of life could apply to our spiritual endeavors as well.

. . . .

But why should Job feel that his anxiety remains hidden from God? In a way his suffering would be more bearable if God did not exist and if he were the sole author of his misfortune. When God no longer hears, why should we keep on speaking?

Divine compassion should lead us to reassurance and not to distress. Instead, we fail to assess properly our existential situations when they are severed from divine mystery. Thus, we ache internally because we prove unable to produce the framework where God can interact with our suffering.

Job has undertaken the journey in search of divine consolation in the land of desolation. He has to learn that God may not be moved by his misfortunes, and that God is not bound to pay attention to the prayers we offer to him. Seldom has any portion of the sacred scriptures come so close to a modern existentialist stance. Job is thrown back upon himself, determining the ways he wants to feel about existence, without any expectation of divine help. He is tortured by such a possibility. His life proclaims the wonders of God. And now, in the throes of injustice and affliction, he could be proven a liar just because he continues to profess that God is not absent from his creation.

Maybe this is not Job's discourse, but Zophar's, later put in Job's mouth. Whatever the case, divine help cannot be tailor-made to suit human situations. This may lead to rebellious or blasphemous conceptions of the divinity. Job finds himself at the edge of his patience with divine indifference. He does not yet know that divine justice does not fail, though it may be delayed beyond our endurance.

If there is a reason for God's silence and indifference, it certainly cannot be understood within the urgency of suffering. Jean Rostand suggests, "The obligation to endure gives us the right to know." In Job's case, the obligation to endure only accentuates the abyss separating him from God and postpones divine consolation. We, too, may have to wait until the day God chooses to put an end to our doubts and to hear our prayers, not according to our desires, but in the context of his fatherly concern, whether we can discern it or not.

Later in the story of Job, after his three friends have failed to silence him, a young man by the name of Elihu appears on the scene and reproaches him for being presumptuous in his requests to God. In his challenge to Job, he reminds him of how easy it is for oppressed people to cry out for help. They seek God only in tragedy, but while healthy and affluent, they forget their maker and fail to perceive his wisdom. God does not answer when they cry out because their lives are fashioned by evil deeds. But what right does Elihu have to compare Job to those whom God refuses to hear? The words of Elihu sound cruel: "Surely God does not hear an empty cry, nor does the Almighty regard it."

What kind of cry would it take to be heard on the other side of emptiness? Can a cry be empty? How can anybody formulate a prayer acceptable to the Lord of all? Sometimes God does not answer our cries, just because they are our cries and do not emanate from an understanding of his will. Oppression has become our lot, and God does not intend to alleviate that side of life. Whatever ails nature, whether known to us or not, must be accepted by those who seek to know divine purpose.

The perspective of Elihu could not comfort Job who is accused of empty talk and a lack of knowledge. It is of course better to approach God in silence than in words. God understands the cry of the heart without our attempt to formulate it. There is no need to explain to God what our prayers are supposed to mean. Only we ourselves are in need of such an explanation, for only we know the pain of oppression. But in and through that oppression, we must encounter the God who can mediate to us all aspects of creation and not just those that, for the moment, affect our lives. Has Job's world become too narrow? When will he know whether his cry will be heard?

. . . .

MEDITATION 45.

Bildad's View of Man (Job 25)

ildad falls victim to a logical but demeaning proposition, namely that God's greatness can be viewed from the point of view of our insignificance. The reduction of life to self-abasement seems to provide religion with a justified foundation. Yet if we were like worms and maggots, as Bildad suggests, then we could look at God only from the vantage point of meaninglessness.

Bildad finds an explanation for Job's misery: the human condition itself, a condition we do not choose, one we cannot alter. The reality of God negates the possibility of the world's perfection. Even the moon and the stars must bear the mark of deficiency in the presence of divine grandeur and excellence.

On occasion we find a similar depreciatory view of human life in the Talmud: "Mark well three things, and you will not fall into the clutches of sin. Know whence you have come, whither you are going, and before whom you are destined to give an account and reckoning. 'Whence have you come?' From a putrid drop. 'Whither are you going?' To a place of dust, worm, and maggot. 'And before whom are you destined to give an account and reckoning?' Before the king of kings, the holy one, blessed be he."

According to Bildad, Job fails to estimate his relative position within the divine economy. Why attempt to become what God forbids us to be in the name of his perfection? But did God need our misery to be conscious of his greatness? If it were so, God's majesty would force religion into a strange dialectic where the lesser is needed to prove the greater. In that case, we could no longer proclaim God's majesty for its own sake.

The less we become, the greater God appears. Such a proposition must contain a radical fallacy. If God introduces human puniness into his creation to prove his greatness, then there is no absolute goodness anywhere, not even in God. Bildad's argument becomes absurd. We need not become worms or maggots to prove divine perfection.

To come to grips with the human condition is to realize that we are poorly equipped to escape our cosmic prison. We have to drag with us millennia of human anxiety and misconduct without the expectation of atoning for the accumulated sins befalling every generation. Our world has produced many silent Jobs whose cries of despair have vanished in the immensity of nothingness. Our short life span makes us even more aware of the distance separating us from the mysteries we attempt to penetrate. God may appear at times remote and inaccessible. Like the Greek philosopher and Sophist Protagoras, we are tempted to conclude that a knowledge of the existence of God lies beyond our intellectual power. The subject is too complex, and life too short to allow us to penetrate such a mystery.

The wonder is that we are capable of thinking and verbalizing God's greatness and eternity. Self-denial may be required to assume the proper religious stance, but it could hardly be the proper vindication for the ultimate purpose of God's creation. If Bildad is not wrong, neither can he be right. We vacillate between the two extremes of misery and grandeur, while God remains immutable.

Because we are not perfect, we must choose the way in which we want to think about ourselves, at times from the point of view of our divine qualities, at other times with the full consciousness of our limitations. The range of religious attitudes is infinite, depending on how close to or far from God we happen to feel we are. The maggot and the worm do not know their maker. But does Bildad? There must be more to Job's plight than God's need to assert his perfection.

Certainly our human race has been involved in enough evils and wrongdoings to feel humbled before God. Still we bear the marks of the divine. Thus, even when conscious of our limitations, we can find ways to celebrate life. Thomas Merton writes, "It is a glorious destiny to be a member of the human race, though it is a race dedicated to many absurdities and one which makes terrible mistakes."

Would Job have agreed with Merton? Would Bildad change his point of view? It is from within our limitations that we learn how to see beyond our restricting horizons, and Job could see much farther in his predicament of suffering than any other person around him. Perhaps he had come to know what Bildad failed to perceive, what later the Talmudic fathers would reiterate: "It is not for us to complete the task, but we have no right to abstain from it."

In his misery, Job came closer to fulfilling the divine purpose than did Bildad with his narrow vision. Since there is more to life than what we can say and know, it may be well to remember the saying of Sophocles: "Nothing that is vast enters into the life of mortals without a curse." His heroes refused to be mere victims of their tragic fate.

. . . .

If there is a curse which is not within human power to escape, neither should mortals succumb to it without a fight for their dignity.

Who shall then know what curses and blessings are, or what they aim at fulfilling within this life? If human greatness brings a curse with it, then we must learn how to change that curse into humble but productive postures. The alternative is complacent nothingness. Bildad chose to emphasize the curse, Job the vastness of the human experience in the incomprehensible context of divine presence.

. . . .

MEDITATION 46.

"He . . . hangs the earth upon nothing." (Job 26:7)

ll religious insights, all systems of belief, all spiritual journeys on a collective or personal level require a certain conception of the created order. Since we share divine space and time, we never cease to wonder about our place within divine purpose.

As was the case for Aristotle and Ptolemy in the Greek-Hellenistic world, the Old Testament produced no acceptable conception of the universe. It was not God's intention to reveal to us the details of his masterwork. For that purpose, he placed in us a searching mind. We participate in the universal miracle that is always close to our heart, yet removed in unspeakable mystery. We feel overcome by what contains us yet eludes our grasp.

Creation's wonders remain fascinating in spite of the inaccuracies of what we perceive about them. The music of the spheres, the harmony of celestial orbs, the divinely inhabited heaven of angels and so many other poetic conceptions of creation still feed our imagination. That which is not accessible to the mind can fill the heart with beauty and bring us closer to our creator. God expects us to see beyond the rational order of the cosmos into the awesome majesty of creation, however mystical it may remain even in a world of scientific knowledge.

Heraclitus knew that nature would always elude us. The more we think we understand it, the more it likes to hide from us. Yet, our yearning for an understanding of the world in which we live will never cease. Job finds it

. . . .

impossible to reflect on God's greatness without formulating a structure for the known world, even as it escapes our comprehension.

In a world where everything reinforces the dichotomy between God's creative powers and our insignificance, we journey back to our origins just to prostrate ourselves in front of our creator who alone can lead us from nothingness to his eternity. And we wonder whether there is a connection between our ephemerality and the world we inhabit. It was in a moment of great soul searching that Job exclaimed, "He . . . hangs the earth upon nothing."

In a thousand different ways the eyes of Job have surveyed the wonders and treasures of creation. Even in his misfortunes he yearns for a knowledge of what he knew would never be revealed to him. He finds peace when he discovers the immediate simplicity of all things. He has suffered devastation and ruin. He has voiced all the reasons for his trials. He has wished to be as far away from God as possible. He has come to know the powers of evil to a greater extent than anybody else. Yet he can now contemplate the sphinxes of his tormented world without being seduced into error or self-pity.

Only in the rudimentary simplicity of faith could Job grasp the multitude of hidden mysteries. He realizes that they were but an infinitesimal part of the whole. In the perspective of death, he contemplates life as never before. His heart and mind no longer search for the refinements of passing tenets. He finds himself immersed in a world floating in the midst of nothingness, yet everywhere revealing God's message. We come closer to God when we learn how to adore him not only for what we see in his creation but also by surmising what is hidden within it.

. . . .

As creatures of a moment, in a cosmos too vast for us to comprehend, we should not attempt to penetrate mysteries which divine wisdom has relegated to the realm of faith. In the fourth century Saint Ambrose suggested that "To discuss the nature and position of the earth does not help us in our hope of the life to come." Persecuted because of his new discoveries in astronomy, Galileo voiced a similar concern, placing faith before science. In a letter to one of his friends he mentions that "The intention of the holy spirit is to teach us how one goes to heaven, not how heaven goes."

Since the truths we know about our world are so few in comparison to those we do not know, we might seek God's presence both in nature and in his word. The apologist Tertullian ended a debate by stating, "We conclude that God is known first through Nature, and then again, more particularly, by doctrine; by Nature in his works, and by doctrine in His revealed word." The earth which hangs upon nothing, adrift among celestial bodies, obeys the perfect divine laws of the cosmos while we search, often in vain, for the anchors which might bring stability to our threatened lives.

So far, Job has been unable to find an acceptable focus for his experience. His journey has led him from order to disorder, a descent into chaos. The divine hand which hangs the earth upon nothing has also allowed the most violent tribulations to take possession of Job's life. Modern science speaks of the world's origin in terms of gigantic cataclysms. The creator's hand was violent, not gentle, and we all bear the marks of that violence. Job has finally understood that his yearning for God's gentleness must lead him to suffering.

We want to question why God hung this earth upon nothing. Why didn't he create a better world? But it is not

. . . .

the time for rational discourse and for a questioning of God's actions. It is not for Job to reproach God for suffering, for turmoil, and for our ignorance of the end of things. The meaning of life comes not from rationality, but from faith. In fact we might be tempted to agree with the modern scientist Steven Weinberg that "The more the universe seems comprehensible, the more it also seems pointless." Job might agree with part of that proposition. Only from the perspective of the end shall we finally know why the earth hangs upon nothing and why we are so unable to understand its meaning.

No science is necessary to understand God's action. His omnipotence and omniscience can make him bring into being what is inconceivable to our minds. He hangs the earth upon nothing. The notion of a void is overpowering. It opposes God's creation from the beginning, but does not hamper it. The void becomes the context of life, the necessary antithesis to life. God alone can utilize it for definite purposes and make it cooperate with his needs.

He hangs the earth upon nothing. No part of creation can float away into nothingness. Thus, even Job's life cannot be in vain. If God can fix the celestial orbs on nothing, then perhaps Job's suffering can also find a point of meaning somewhere. He exists as part of a whole into which he will dissolve again according to a divine purpose that never ceases to baffle him.

The succession of cosmic events and the order of creation testify to God's supremacy. Were he not the source of it all, how would anything have meaning? Job refuses to conceive of any natural phenomenon other than direct divine action. God supervises every detail of the great machine, and nothing escapes his influence. Water cannot become clouds without God's direct impact. Such immanence explains both the goodness and the wrath of God. Being a part of God's world leads Job to know that he must accept suffering in the same way he accepts blessings.

He hangs the earth upon nothing! So we too hang upon nothing. We can stop at any moment and contemplate the wondrous works of the creator. The world we inhabit cannot contain him. Our minds are not powerful or worthy enough to celebrate him as we should. We are destined to remember our insignificance until we discover the divine love which encircles us. The greatest majestic rivers of the world begin as small trickles before they grow into impressive bodies of water making their way through the splendors of creation.

Like the earth, Job's life hangs upon nothing. Perhaps absolute nothingness would have been better than the torments of earthly life. The destiny of Job in God's economy baffles our mind. When all was denied him, he was made into a proclaimer of value, meaning, and purpose amid despair, doubt, and discouragement. The question was no longer what kind of earth God hangs upon nothing, but whether in that very nothingness we can find the spiritual anchors that will guide us safely into eternity.

. . . .

MEDITATION 47.

"As long as my breath is in me." (Job 27:3)

he ultimate standard of evaluation in life finds its summary in a simple yet powerful proposition: as long as there is breath in us we are animated by God's spirit. Certainly the clay was a poor receptacle for it and provided the blueprint for disasters to follow. But it was God's choice, and it was divine life that was poured into the earthen vessel. It is in the nature of things that the vessel not question its content.

Job finds himself again at a mystifying crossroads in his thinking. His contention with God must proceed in the name of fairness. There is no logical explanation of the fact that God has taken away his rights and thrown bitterness into his soul. Yet until the day of his death, he knows that his existence depends on the continuous breath of life dispensed by the creator. That thought never fails to be sobering. Any rebellion against God is a rebellion against ourselves.

Beyond the peaceful confines of the Garden of Eden, good and evil brought fragmentation and disintegration to the breath of life, God's greatest gift to his children. In every human breath there is part of God's breath. In every thought there is part of divine purpose. In every discouragement there is part of the universal sadness of a creation gone astray. Whatever Job can say, feel, speak, deny, hope, curse, or bless is possible only because of God's breath in him. Therefore he is overcome by a sense of responsibility toward his soul as he resolves to remain

. . . .

a moral servant of God, beyond reproach in his speech and thinking. Yet we find in Job the surprising claim that he knows how to discriminate between good and evil and not let his life be dragged into falsehood and deceit.

For a moment, Job's thoughts wander outside himself. He becomes conscious of the bewildering universality of the breath of God shared by countless wanderers through existence who, like him, may fail to praise the Lord of creation. His personal experience loses its unique character. There are many people in the world who suffer what he suffers, who pray what he prays, who hope what he hopes.

Even in his misery Job realizes that he is a part of the suffering world to which he must bring hope and comfort: "Did I not weep for him whose day was hard? Was not my soul grieved for the poor?" Thus, as Ambrose suggests, we should no longer wonder at the judgment of God in the case of Job. Rather we should wonder at his virtue when he remembers in his misfortune the blessing he was for others in times of prosperity: "I was eyes to the blind, and feet to the lame. I was a father to the poor, and I searched out the cause of him whom I did not know."

A touch of the spirit! A touch of that which is other than ourselves, a touch of that which does not allow itself to be easily touched. And in all of it we fail, sometimes because we seek for great things that do not exist. Not all of us are called upon to do great things. Those may be reserved for God or for his servants such as Job, Moses, Jacob, the prophets, or the saints. Our contribution may consist in transforming small things until we see in them the larger picture of life and discover that behind the turmoil, the activities, the frustrations of

. . . .

worldly business, there is a place for peace, for serenity, for rest, for quietness, for redemption.

A touch of the spirit! How could Job listen to his heart, mostly when he tried to let it be filled with God's presence? How could he unlearn the things that kept him riveted to wrong thoughts, and how could he learn the beauty and dangers of a freedom and duty to himself and to others?

Much too often we cannot add a touch of the spirit, for there is no proper receptacle to contain it. Spirituality has become a difficult word to explain, for it can neither be comprehended nor translated into definite propositions. It changes with each individual, and the greatest mistake would consist in levelling its meaning to what is acceptable to all.

Job avoids falling prey to the advice of friends and loved ones when he feels that that advice is out of step with his inner resonance. The spirit never conforms to stereotype, and we cannot copy our spiritual life from others. They may serve as models, but there is a personal touch of the spirit that defines our being. Paradoxically, the touch of the spirit may be hard to discover, for God never reveals to us the full extent of our potential. How far then can we go on the path leading to him?

The God who gives and takes away has also assigned limits to the breath of life which will remain within us until it reintegrates its original source. For Job, the blessed are those who turn God's gift into righteous living, while the others frustrate God's purpose by using the same gift for the wrong ends. Whatever his suffering, Job ceases to contend with God when he remembers that without God's breath in him, he would not even partake of existence.

. . . .

There is a nobility in Job that has served as a lesson to us: It is more honorable to suffer injustice than to perpetrate it, even when contending with God. In his misfortune, Job prefers to keep his integrity: "I hold fast to my righteousness, and will not let it go." Is Job conceited? Perhaps. But he has already suffered enough to perceive what righteousness entails. Heavenly powers may have been right. There is none like him. Has the breath of God, in this particular case, made him equal to God in determination and perseverance? Satan was able to persuade God. Would he have the same success with Job? Satan has certainly chosen the wrong representative of the human race to win his wager.

Whatever else redemption may mean, it requires that we cherish the power of God's life-giving breath in us so that, like Job, we may be spared from error and from the search for a facile solution to what remains incomprehensible. "As long as my breath is in me, and the spirit of God is in my nostrils; my lips will not speak falsehood, and my tongue will not utter deceit."

MEDITATION 48.

Job's Hymn of Wisdom. (Job 28)

Wisdom presupposes knowledge of the self, a state Job would have liked to achieve. To present himself before God with a clear conscience remained a goal he swore not to abandon until death. Has he reached wisdom? Where is it to be found? Job knows that it is not a result of human achievements. It is exclusively of divine origin and cannot be communicated through knowledge. "But where shall wisdom be found? And where is the place of understanding? Man does not know the way to it, and it is not found in the hands of the living." Yet, it is all around us in the manifold expressions of God's work. It is as if we were destined to live in its presence without being able to make it our own.

According to the apocryphal book *Wisdom of Solomon*, wisdom comes to us in a sincere desire for instruction which leads to love and then to immortality. In the presence of wisdom, Solomon was supposed to have said, "I learned without guile and I impart without grudging: I do not hide wisdom's wealth, for it is an unfailing treasure for men; those who get it obtain friendship with God, commended for the gifts that come from instruction. May God grant that I speak with judgment and have thoughts worthy of what I have received, for he is the guide even of wisdom and the corrector of the wise."

The universality of wisdom clashes with the temporality of the human condition. In another apocryphal

. . . .

book, the *Wisdom of Jesus the Son of Sirach,* we find one of the most lofty praises of the eternity of wisdom: "I [wisdom] came forth from the mouth of the Most High, and covered the earth like a mist. I dwelt in high places, and my throne was in a pillar of cloud. Alone I have made the circuit of the vault of heaven and have walked in the depth of the abyss. . . . From eternity, in the beginning, God created me, and for eternity I shall not cease to exist."

In the days of Job, wisdom had become the servant of technology, and he was quite willing to recognize the multifaceted benefits of human ingenuity. He demonstrated a mastery of information concerning the ways in which his contemporaries exploited the resources of the earth and turned them to their advantage. But there was no wisdom in any of that, save human propensity to claim glory and progress, which need not be in harmony with God's purpose.

In the ancient world, the mining of ore became linked with survival and required highly developed skills to avoid mortal danger. Wisdom had to match nature's tenacity. What was hidden deep within the earth became a challenge to human inventiveness, but also, much too often, the cause of misery and death. Mining has always carried with it a daring against which nature arises with a vengeance.

When I was fourteen, I started working in the coal mines in northern France. In the very mine where I worked, well over a thousand workers had died many decades earlier in a methane explosion on March 10, 1906. Conscious of such danger, I wrote in my journal, "In the depths of the earth! Coal mining! Pride of the brave and challenge of the daring! A strange and harsh relationship

. . . .

exists between that which does not want to yield and the human determination to dislodge it from its peaceful resting place. Nature does not allow itself to be wounded without inflicting pain, injury, or even death on the transgressors. Physical suffering matches the turmoil of the mind and the fear of the heart. Our imprint on nature becomes irreversible. Depleted empty tunnels crisscross subterranean geography while newly formed black mountains reshape the landscape above. Mortal danger accompanies me at every moment in a job no one would choose if not by absolute necessity. From the peaceful fields of the countryside to the pervasive threats of a work place that could become my tomb at any moment, who will ever understand what determines my destiny? Darkness by night and darkness by day, darkness inside and darkness outside! It becomes everybody's responsibility to comprehend properly the limits within which we can progress or end, for mercy does not abound in the depths of the earth where human intrusion is not welcomed." Nature's revenge exceeds our wisdom.

The Book of Job has given us a description of astonishing technical abilities of *homo faber* in the exploitation of natural resources. But the praise of intelligence cannot hide the bitter truth that the ultimate secret of the world cannot be revealed to us. True wisdom is hidden from all living creatures. Understanding consists in departing from evil, and wisdom resides in the fear of the Lord. No ability to mine ore and refine it can equate or replace the only source of wisdom which consists of a proper relationship to creation. Wisdom lacks heroes, for few ever come to discover it.

Throughout the centuries, the people of God had been confronted with many versions of wisdom, mostly

. . . .

the Babylonian brand which the Jews espoused in the Exile. But there was also the Greek version which deeply influenced Western culture and the Oriental perspective which correlates with mysticism. What indeed is wisdom? *The Wisdom of Solomon* provides this definition: "Wisdom is a breath of the power of God, and a pure emanation of the glory of the Almighty; therefore nothing defiled gains entrance into her. For she is a reflection of eternal light, a spotless mirror of the workings of God, and an image of his goodness."

Wisdom implies transcendence. It sits in judgment over our lives and compels us to seek for more than the satisfaction of material goods. Wisdom is a divine quality we are called upon to share with God. It commends us to our creator, though we may never know exactly what it is. In humility it inhabits holy souls, friends of God, and prophets of the Lord. It is the source of perpetual paradox, for only fools can claim to possess it. Those who feel removed from it are the closest to it.

The Book of Job teaches us that what comes out of daily necessity pulls us down and leads us away from transcendence. According to Eskimo lore, "wisdom can be found only far from man, out in the great loneliness." By nature it removes itself from mediocrity. What then is the meaning of wisdom we acquire in loneliness? Is it possible that wisdom is not meant to be shared with others? It rests on a personal experience of life not readily visible outside of its repository. The wisdom of Job is the wisdom of a lone traveler not swayed by the judgment of others, by their approval or condemnation. It is the foundation of every decision and action which meets with the approbation of conscience.

. . . .

As in the case of Job, it is worth our while to pause in the midst of adversity and to contemplate the meaning of life at a time when everything is taken away from us. But our world is too engrossed in technological progress to hear the voice of wisdom. From Job to the present, the world has not changed much. Few are those who search for wisdom. Fewer still are those who find it. At one point Job allowed himself to sink into pessimism and view his contemporaries as the killers of wisdom: "No doubt you are the people, and wisdom will die with you."

MEDITATION 49.

Times to Be Remembered. (Job 29)

"n all adversity of misfortune, the most wretched kind is once to have been happy," said Boethius in a situation not so dissimilar to Job's. Memory can provide a pause in our misfortunes. To remember can be joyous or sad. For Job, the blessings of the past appear greater now that he must contemplate them from his perspective of desolation. How can the same God dispense favors and misery without explanation?

For Job, once to have been happy also means that life is not devoid of ultimate meaning. Specific experiences can be immortalized and rescued from the vicissitudes of earthly existence. Traveling back through time does not always comfort us in our suffering, but it might help us restore our equilibrium. One must learn how to remember good times and how to forget some of the unavoidable misery. Loren Eiseley suggests, "There are two diametrically opposed forces forever at war in the heart of man: one is memory; the other is forgetfulness. No one knows completely the nature of the inner turmoil which creates this struggle."

What does memory consist of? Is there, as sometimes suggested, a happy and an unhappy memory? Time gives memory its eclectic nature, and sometimes we do not know why we remember some things while we forget others. We do not always control our memories. God alone remembers all. But to what end and for what purpose?

. . . .

Thus far Job has not been able to come to grips with his own feelings. Now that the friendship of God is no longer upon his tent, why not abandon hope and avoid the grief of fate? Was Boethius more perceptive than Job? Doesn't remembrance of past happiness increase the sorrow of the present when one is thrown into suffering? Yet it is precisely in suffering that Job remembers with joy his past actions, especially when he could be of help to the bereaved and the dispossessed. There is virtue in not letting the affliction of the moment take away or diminish the blessings of the past. Part of ourselves does not change, and part of ourselves remains in constant turmoil. Wisdom connects the two into a single being.

Both Boethius and Job were stricken at the height of their physical and spiritual powers. So, they lacked the consolation of old age or the rationalization of life's inexorable movement toward death. When everything is taken away, memory alone can maintain a sense of place and time. To forget is to die, to remember is to create meaning. The Greeks knew that when they made the goddess of memory, Mnemosyne, the mother of the muses. The Hebrews felt it deeply in their exile from the land as they gathered by the waters of Babylon and wept for their holy city of Jerusalem. They knew that to forget was to lose their collective identity. To remember is to vindicate God's purpose which alone connects our origins and our ends.

Sometimes we stare at life as a painter may view the blank canvas. In the temporal process, things may remain flat and colorless, lacking depth and dimension. Yet through the creative power of the mind, we can impress on the flat canvas our tragedies or joys, translating them into multidimensional realities that will survive our

. . . .

intentions. What we imprint on the canvas of our lives becomes a part of human and divine memory. When divine will and human will agree on what should be recorded, we enter the process of redemption.

Memory allows us to leave our footprints on the sands of time. The human wilderness need not be empty of meaning. Great men and women of the past have marked trails in it for us to follow. But the winds of time have blown the sand back into their footprints, and we must patiently reconstruct the road to follow. In the process we may choose our companions, those who like Job have been where we might never go. They may warn us of the dangers or prepare us for the joys of the journey. The worst would be to forget and never become a part of the eternal picture.

The wisdom of the ages provides no answer to the riddle of our present situation. We keep the memory of eternity while bound by time. We dream of immortality while accepting the end of our mortal selves. Cicero suggested that we recognize God because we remember the source from which we sprang. We can contemplate with serenity or with sadness the moments in our lives that remind us of all the transformations time imposes on our being.

In memory there is also unhappiness, for the truly happy person would need no memory, just the intensity of the moment. Forgetting might be as great a virtue as remembering, mostly when we refuse to introduce into our lives the visions of misery brought by the passage of time. At the end the spirit returns to God, free from the burdens of a negative memory. The rest no longer counts. Fears and anxieties, though unavoidable, are not made of

. . . .

that which lasts. Why then are they so predominant in life? Is it to keep us alert to the possibility that we might lose sight of the essential while burdened by the trivial? If there is the coming of an evil day, then the rest of our days should be devoted to lessen as much as possible the impact of such an event through all the goodness that can be generated in our lives.

What else does Job have but the memory of a glorious life? Should that perish because it no longer has an immediate existence? Is the soul emptied of things that once dwelt in it? That which we consider lost within our lives need not be annihilated within God's memory. We shall all be deprived of what was ours during our lifetime. But we shall carry with us the memory of things that can be remolded into permanent worth.

When memory tends to fade, God compels us to turn our gaze toward the milestones on our path as reminders of the journey we have completed and as signs of the distance separating us from his eternity. Misfortune is blind because it intensifies the present and cannot concern itself with past or future. Job knows the weight of his predicament, but for a moment he has allowed himself a small glance back into happiness. Without surmising it, he also gained a glimpse into the future.

. . . .

MEDITATION 50.

The words of Job are ended. (Job 31:40)

he time has come for Job to know silence, the condition produced either by wisdom or exhaustion. From personal distress to universal injustice, Job has now journeyed through the land of desolation where even the most genuine of words could no longer convey the essence of being. All dialogue has reached an end for lack of focus.

When God's creation appears absurd, and when even the most righteous person of all is condemned to live within it deprived of the knowledge of its purpose, silence may be preferable to indignation. If words still mean anything, they relate to the past rather than to the present. Before ending his speech, Job reached back into his life when he was a successful being. In all religious and moral situations, he proved to be a person of high ethical sensitivity. That conviction compelled him to speak loud, in fact loud enough to believe that God must now listen: "Therefore I will not restrain my mouth; I will speak in the anguish of my spirit; I will complain in the bitterness of my soul." But no more. There comes a time when speech is no longer useful.

Here is my signature, says Job, by definition the last word of any written document, the word which guarantees authenticity. It is written with pride and self-confidence, in the form of a prince who fears not his station in life. Will God answer now that Job no longer speaks? When we have said all that is humanly possible,

. . . .

does that compel God to pay attention? Job does not yet know. It is enough for him to have reviewed his life and to be able to present it to God in an irreproachable fashion. If Job cannot be delivered from his misfortune by his just and moral behavior, where then is the answer? Or is Job's plight the fact that he does not have at his disposal words which could open new doors in his dialogue with God? How many words does one need to deal with things eternal and divine?

Without realizing it, Job has begun to frustrate God's plan. How could God pursue the wager if the major character refuses to cooperate? Has God given special heed to the limits of human endurance? Job's silence will compel the rapid movement toward a final resolution. Our temporality and the brevity of life do not allow us to create words which would ensure transcendence. Job has reached his own conclusion. He can pronounce his innocence and find the right words to proclaim it. If God's words must dominate in biblical religion, so also human words must be taken seriously by God. And where words no longer exist, silence may well frustrate divine intentions. The words of Job are ended. Soon all of his story will also end, only to become the parable of the suffering community spread throughout the world, with its boundless sea of tragedy and its relentless search for a divine anchor in the midst of turbulent and destructive waves.

God, however, did not allow a stalemate. Time after time the words of Job clashed with those of his friends whose arguments reached the point of exhaustion. For a moment the wager appeared threatened, and certainly God could not allow Satan to have the satisfaction of seeing Job defeated. The tribulation had to go on.

. . . .

It continued through the intrusion into the story of a clever and self-confident debater by the name of Elihu. He must stir Job into a new consciousness of his situation and forbid him to believe that all contention with God must cease. "Be silent, and I will teach you wisdom," proposes Elihu to Job.

Who will teach wisdom to whom? Are there not times when we would rather avoid the company of self-righteous teachers who have no insight into our plight? Does the poetic verve of Elihu contain anything that Job does not already know through his suffering? The kind of silence Elihu suggests does not find a proper place in a life of turmoil. Creation cries out for vindication and justification. When evil destroys innocent beings, it is not time for acquiescence but for indignation. Elihu may have found himself in the position of an armchair philosopher offering advice without knowing the pain of being.

Job finds himself at the end of a long journey through physical and mental anguish. He was blessed with caring friends. They were the voice of wisdom. They collected, summarized, and interpreted all possible reasons for the existence of events beyond their understanding. Their wisdom was not in silence but in speech, in an effort to share what they had learned about life and about God. It did not produce the expected results. Elihu's conviction that he has found a new approach will lead to anger rather than comfort.

Elihu is right in his first proposition: to know wisdom one must be silent. But he errs on the second proposition: that wisdom can be taught. Wisdom is deeply personal and cannot be communicated, for we each possess our own brand of it. The wise person never claims to possess

. . . .

wisdom, for it abandons you the very moment you are convinced of having achieved it.

Elihu's wisdom, if we can call it that, could hardly prove redemptive to Job. Yet, it can and must test Job's wisdom. Now that the words of Job have ended, will he still listen to the words of others, especially those of Elihu? Job's situation will not be altered until God intervenes. Then all words of wisdom will be annihilated.

What kind of wisdom is it that Elihu can teach? And does Job really need it? In a cosmos that tends to deny ultimate order and meaning, we are bound to seek our own wisdom and fill the void of God's distance. Job has now learned the power of silence. But has he become wise? Perplexed by a story which refused to fit any rational scheme, the medieval Jewish philosopher Maimonides concluded that Job was a good man, but not a wise one. Perhaps it was faith, not wisdom, that gave meaning to the wager and to the way in which Job responded to it.

MEDITATION 51.

The Anger of Elihu. (Job 32)

trange indeed that a newcomer to the story would find no other response than anger at Job and his friends. Job could no longer assess his relationship to God, and his friends were unable to bring him any comfort. Everything was recast in a mode of thought that could not fit into the expectations of Elihu. We heard from childhood that God's main purpose is to bring order into chaotic lives. But the story of Job fails to vindicate religious tenets which, for so long, have been regarded as unassailable.

The impetuous young Elihu does not concern himself with the particular circumstances of Job's life or with the inability of his friends to find answers to his plight. He stands there with a message, with the conviction of his righteousness. In his eyes, Job has departed from acceptable behavior by justifying himself rather than God. True enough! Job's suffering has generated a heightened consciousness of himself. Wasn't the purpose of God's wager that Job should serve him even in the worst of times?

The end of the story of Job surprises us. Job had endured so much. Why does God put on his path a young impulsive person who can respond to the situation only with anger? How much are we willing to learn from anger? There is something frightening about human anger, an unconscious response to deep psychological disturbances which lie beyond the control of most people, a call to the irrational and the vengeful, and often

. . . .

the cause of a useless tragedy. Not many days pass without some reminder of that in the news.

On a deeper level, anger is an essential quality we share with God. The Old Testament mentions hundreds of instances when God is angry at his creation and at his people. But there is a way in which anger is not connected with what we call sin, otherwise God himself would be guilty of it. Did Paul think of that when he wrote, "Be angry but do not sin; do not let the sun go down on your anger"? In some instances it may require quite a long day.

What would life be without anger, divine or human? Why are we destined to share it with God? If the divine essence is not free of it, how can we expect to control it on our earthly plane? Most of the tragedies of our world come from the fact that many decisions are made in the context of anger. The reputed scholar of Tarsus advised Caesar that, if angry, he should repeat the alphabet several times before saying anything. By that time, anger would have subsided to make room for more rational decisions.

No one can totally avoid anger, but some of us can recognize its deleterious consequences. It never achieves the goals expected. It exhibits the highest level of disrespect for anything that is human in others and often in ourselves. Certainly there are reasons why we should be angry at some points, and we could justify that anger. We could reproach Elihu for his anger. But we should also remember that Job is not free of it.

It is difficult to be compassionate and recognize in others what may be lacking in ourselves. We shall never see the end of the pain inflicted by the self-righteous, for they have lost sight of their own failures and limitations. Anger is an expression of weakness, an inability to

. . . .

know oneself in the human condition, a shortcut to gain that which we cannot secure through respect and dignity. But somehow it never works and leaves everybody threatened and diminished.

Anger remains our companion in a journey through the contradictions we encounter without being able to consign them to their proper place. To a certain degree, it can be turned toward its own object. We have the capacity to be angry at ourselves, though we would call such a feeling indignation.

Most of the time, anger is directed at others. The greatest of mysteries, namely that we are all different, turns out to be a liability when it stands in the way of our expectations. When what is advantageous and convenient for others clashes with our views of conduct, we tend to assert what we believe to be true, consequently what, in our view, everybody should agree on. But anger comes from the fact that we never encounter the world with the totality of our being, but with fragments and pieces we understand to be a totality, though it cannot be.

We must appreciate our ability to distinguish between good and evil, moral and immoral, regardless of whether or not we are accurate in our estimation of those situations. For in the final analysis, we must rule the world of events by our capacity to think, to feel, and to love. It is not always possible to know who the winners and the losers are. When we elevate our relative standards to absolutes, we throw the world into turmoil and ourselves into anger. Elihu proves incapable of considering that his beliefs, not Job's, are wrong.

Then here comes our major problem, for it is not desirable that we live permanently in meaningless relativity.

. . . .

Somewhere there must be universal norms of morality and spirituality. But are we really the judges of what they are? And do we have the right to expect others to adopt our beliefs about them? Whoever we are, we are prone to arrogance. No one has ever been able to overcome that liability completely.

Perhaps the best advice comes from Marcus Aurelius who points out that we cannot expect to satisfy our anger by proving ourselves right, for that would be at the expense of the essential being of others, who have the same right to the same position. But we might, if strong enough, teach ourselves and others that not all things which are congenial and advantageous are right. If we can enter such a learning process, we may win the battle against anger.

The Greeks liked to propose that wisdom resides in knowing oneself, a point we reach through careful analysis and rational activity. No such avenue was open to Job. He came to know himself, but only through intense suffering and incomprehensible events. Elihu does not yet have any insight into the other side of God, thus his anger. He has not yet realized that we should not disturb God's universe except when God himself chooses to throw everything into turmoil.

Elihu's anger should be directed to God, not Job. If Job has found a way to justify himself, it must be put to his credit, to his power to remain human when confronted with divine fury. Elihu does not have, for the time being, the insight to realize that when Job justifies himself, he does indeed justify God, for what was at stake was not Job's life, but God's wager about it. None of his friends could solve such a puzzle. They had no satisfactory answers despite their noble intentions. In his anger Elihu could not even surmise that he was proposing wrong answers. In the final analysis Job alone was part of the experiment, not his friends, and not Elihu. Since Job's words came to an end, why not give him the peace of his solitariness? Elihu offered beautiful poems in the hope of being more successful than Job's friends. But his self-righteousness about his own convictions did not allow him to perceive that God was not likely to let human wisdom gain the upper hand in a wager no one understood, not even Job.

. . . .

MEDITATION 52.

"'Job speaks without knowledge, his words are without insight.'" (Job 34:35)

hen one surveys religion from a human point of view, one finds human essence in it, more than divine otherness. The poetic verve of Elihu has conjured up numerous images of righteousness and virtue, and Job has failed every standard applied to him. When the divine encounters the human, even poetic imagination fails to comprehend the magnitude of the mystery.

The right of Job to rebel against God does not fit Elihu's concept of religion according to which all creatures must bow unconditionally in the presence of God. But Job has discovered a truth not available to Elihu, namely that in a world ravaged by sin and satanic forces one finds God only in an essential act of rebellion. One does not solve the problems of this world by becoming a small, obedient vassal, for that would be conspiring with the forces of evil. Quite the contrary. God awaits us in conflicts which appear to be beyond our strength. Heraclitus said that Polemos, the god of war, is both king and father of all, disclosing who is godlike and who is but a slave. Christ stunned his hearers when he warned them that he did not come to bring peace but the sword.

Job's spiritual quest goes far beyond Elihu's world view. Elihu has become guilty of a universal sin, that of belittling or condemning what he cannot understand. Reducing everything to the few propositions with which one feels comfortable has been the innate tendency of people who seek security of belief. The accusation that Job speaks without knowledge reflects more on Elihu than on Job.

There is a knowledge which passes all understanding, and because it is not accessible to the human mind, it remains in the realm of our surmise and faith. To a certain degree, we all speak without knowledge, for what we term knowledge allows us only a limited view into divine mysteries. Our communion with God depends more on faith than on knowledge. Growing in wisdom and faith does not always mean that we know more. It may sometimes require that we abandon some forms of knowledge. Why then does Elihu feel the need to approach Job with such self-righteousness? He speaks from a position of ignorance, for he knows nothing about the wager. In reality, neither does Job.

The drama played out in Job is not intended to impugn or exonerate either God or Job but to stress that where evil forces are unleashed, creation stands in need of redemption. But no one ever finds redemption in reflection alone. The idea that through suffering we participate with God in the struggle against evil escapes Elihu and, at some point, also Job. Perfect understanding and faultless insights, if they were available to us, would provide flawless solutions. Elihu has simply failed to admit that no human mind, not even his own, can contend for understanding in a world sustained by principles that God did not disclose to us. The irony is that he is right in his criticism of Job. But he is not wise enough to know that his self-assurance and reasoning, together with his beautiful poetic verve, remain of human origin and do not mirror God's intention and purpose.

Job becomes the tragic hero and the cathartic representative of a humankind which can receive salvation

. . . .

only in a vicarious way. He is the image of the Old Testament saint through whose suffering, divine grace can be extended to others. But before we experience divine grace, we must journey to the source of turmoil and instability. Poetic craft can make our situations more bearable, but it cannot redeem them. In some ways, Job's rebellion and Elihu's poetry belong together, though neither of them yet knows it.

MEDITATION 53.

"God is great, and we know him not." (Job 36:26)

ur propensity for extolling the virtues of the mind is often challenged by our awareness of ignorance. In his self-confidence Elihu can proclaim great truths even when distorted by personal motives. He assumes to know what Job ignores, namely how to approach God. Tradition is on his side. One can hardly read the speeches of Elihu without being moved by their depth and by his praise of the splendors of nature. Everything within God's providence invites us to celebrate life. Why then is it of so little comfort to Job?

There is an assumption in Elihu that, on the surface, commends itself to our rationality and intelligence. The common voice of humankind has agreed on the majesty of creation. Consequently we should extol the works of God of which people of the past have sung. In doing so, we shall find the right way to God, though he may remain beyond our reach.

There seems to be little wrong with a theology that invites Job to "stop and consider the wondrous works of God." It is rather unexpected that, right after the poetic descriptions of Elihu, God appears to Job not in the glory of creation but out of the whirlwind with a powerful rebuke: "The Lord answered Job out of the whirlwind: who is this that darkens counsel by words without knowledge?"

We may feel threatened in our religion when traditions fail to renew our spiritual strength. There

. . . .

was nothing wrong in what Elihu said, except perhaps that he had reached a point of feeling secure in his religious knowledge. Here is a tacit reminder that, because we cannot know God in his fullness, we should reject that which gives us a sense of absolute certainty. To live in the presence of God is to remain in awe. When we have learned our lessons well, even those we can attribute to the scriptures, we may have reached not the point of knowledge but the point of trained ignorance, a fact Jesus never stopped contending about with the Pharisees.

In disarming simplicity, Job could admit the power of the forces of ignorance. The enemy of the heart resisted the process of taming. Job did not even know where to start the demolition of biases and prejudices. He was fortunate to have intelligent friends, just to find out that their wisdom was of no avail. Socrates arose against trained ignorance in favor of a hidden knowledge, and Christ invited his hearers to discover the power of the kingdom within themselves. Our ignorance makes our worlds seem larger than they are. I recall a statement of Marshall Mcluhan that could apply to the religious world as well as to the scientific one: "Every new discovery opens up vast areas of ignorance."

How does one measure the greatness of what one does not know? Elihu has entered into a long description of God's wonders as they are revealed in the works of creation, especially the seasons of the year. Does Elihu think that the suffering of Job is the result of his inability to grasp the majesty of the creator?

In the midst of God's great works, one wonders and marvels, one does not question and search the unknowable. Have we then come this far in Job's journey just to conclude that it was ill-conceived and useless? The

. . . .

courage to question God's deeds does not fit into Elihu's theology, and for the moment he seems to have the upper hand over Job.

Here also lies a great paradox. Our ability to know the works of nature comes from a source that cannot be clearly identified. The knowledge that enables us to form our concepts of the divine also reminds us of the limits within which it can be utilized. We cannot know God, for to know something is to be able to define it clearly and fully. How then does one escape the burden of ignorance? Aristotle provided a simple, and sometimes elusive answer: The true love of wisdom resides in perpetual contemplation. We can always flee to our own country, suggested Agamemnon in Homer's poems. Plotinus, Gregory, and Augustine changed that saying by showing how we can always go home to ourselves and find there the riches God has hidden in our being.

In a poignant summary of a journey that should have led the people to choose life over death, Moses challenged those who wandered through the wilderness to find within themselves the law of God: "For this commandment which I command you this day is not too hard for you, neither is it far off. It is not in heaven, that you should say, 'Who will go up for us to heaven, and bring it to us, that we may hear it and do it?' Neither is it beyond the sea, that you should say, 'Who will go over the sea for us, and bring it to us, that we may hear it and do it?' But the word is very near you; it is in your mouth and in your heart, so that you can do it."

The closer we come to God, the more shaken our lives may appear as we cross from knowledge to faith. As a young religious person who studied at the feet of the great rabbi Gamaliel, Saul of Tarsus became so convinced

. . . .

of his righteousness that he could, in the name of God, persecute those who did not agree with him. As a mature Christian, he reflected on his past life and said, "I received mercy because I acted ignorantly in unbelief, and the grace of our Lord overflowed for me with the faith and love that are in Christ Jesus." Somehow, as we grow older and choose the way of wisdom, we become more tolerant and more compassionate. At least we should.

My first invitation to visit the United States, before it became my permanent home, consisted of a speaking tour. Most of my addresses centered on a comparison between European and American religious practices. I recall how at the beginning of the tour I felt secure in my knowledge of what I had read and learned about the United States. A few weeks after my arrival, I began to have some doubts about what I was saying. Now, after many years of residency and citizenship in the United States, I would not even attempt any final pronouncements on the subject.

But then think of Job again. He is not interested in Elihu's or anybody else's theology. He has a knowledge that does not come from formal learning. For Job, one knows through the totality of being, through an intimate relationship. Is that not, after all, how knowledge is described in the Old Testament, the very Yadah Yahweh?

Theology cannot be learned in schools or seminaries alone, however indispensable they may be, but through the act of living. "And this is eternal life, that they may know thee, the only true God," is the best description of knowledge we received from Christ himself. Knowledge is life, and life is knowledge, and when we extend both beyond the temporal, we meet God. No doubt, the transitoriness of everything that surrounds us belies the unity and eternity of the whole. Yet peace and serenity can be acquired through our ability to transcend the temporary and view life in the perspective of eternity.

Perhaps we err in our belief that God sets up precise goals and purposes for us to fulfill. If that had been the case with Job, he might have avoided his distress. It is difficult to approach every new day with fresh questions. We cannot easily overcome our tendency toward organization and a sense of having done what is expected of us. True religion begins beyond that level, in the realm of faith, in the openness to the unknown, in a journey with God that has no end and is not subject to our human maps, in the slow maturation which allows us to cross from temporality to eternity and from life to immortality. The late Lewis Thomas wrote, "We are ignorant about how we work, about where we fit in, and most of all about the enormous imponderable system of life in which we are embedded as working parts. We do not really understand nature, at all. We have come a long way indeed, but just enough to become conscious of our ignorance." I have often reflected on that saying and the impact it has had on my own spiritual journey.

Our world is too small to contain God. Our minds are too limited to conceive of him in any ultimate way. But that should not concern us. Only at the end of the journey did Job come to know that the striving alone reveals the meaning of life. The gift of knowledge was not intended to reinforce our limited horizons, but for us to reach toward what is unattainable. How long will it take us to realize that our claims to knowledge are nothing but a refusal to admit our limitations? In a genuine spiritual journey, knowledge and faith can no longer be separated.

. . . .

MEDITATION 54.

The L*ORD* *answered Job out of the whirlwind. (Job 38:1)*

he whirlwind—the colliding of opposing forces giving rise to turbulence and tumultuous events! Job has exhausted himself in his attempt to understand his situation. All kinds of advice, criticism, and judgment have come from his friends. Yet, no real answer to his situation has been found. The whirlwind grew larger and stronger. Neither the mind nor the heart could rise up to meet the void and the despair. So it was God's turn to speak and to manifest himself.

Job had endured enough, and God alone could enter a situation no longer manageable on the human plane. God reappeared on the scene abruptly, cutting off all human words he had tolerated to that time. For much too long points of view clashed with each other, and human wisdom derailed the proper search for God's intentions. What is it that we come to know at the end, after we have said all that is humanly possible?

Out of the whirlwind! Out of the accumulation of theories, beliefs, dogmas, hopes, and illusions! The whole of life is a whirlwind, a search for the unknown and the impossible, a confrontation between the ideal and the real, the urge for life in an environment intent on destroying it, the advice of friends which turns out to be nefarious. A whirlwind of our own creation, though God contributed to it greatly in Job. But the answer must come, and Job must be prepared to receive it.

. . . .

Neither on his own nor with the help of his friends has Job been able to identify the whirlwind of his turmoil. Now he must enter another whirlwind, one whose source is God himself, one that comes from heaven and returns to heaven. It was the same whirlwind which appeared in troubled times and carried the chariot of Elijah into heaven, a whirlwind which denied death its power and grip on the beloved prophet.

Job must stand revealed. He can no longer keep to himself his anxieties and his fears. It has taken the voice of the whirlwind and the decision of God to break his silence, to make Job aware of the true nature of the chaos that has distorted everything in his life for much too long. He must hear God proclaim a truth that eluded him in his stubborn quest. Heaven and earth refused to disclose the laws affecting divine creation. Job must journey back to the beginning of things, to the chaos as it was before God changed it into order. Where was Job when it all happened? Perhaps chaos is not yet totally subdued. The leviathans still roam God's creation, and Job must know what it means.

As long as the whirlwind affects only others, we can be thankful for the dangers we do not have to experience. Like the friends of Job, we can watch them from a safe physical or spiritual distance. While pondering the nature of things, Lucretius wrote, "How sweet it is, when whirlwinds roil great oceans, to watch, from land, the dangers of another. Not that to see some other person suffer brings great enjoyment. But the sweetness lies in watching evils you yourself are free from."

But soon Lucretius warned that whirlwinds cannot be escaped forever: "O wretched minds of men! O hearts in darkness! Under what shadows and among what dangers

. . . .

your lives are spent, such as they are. But look—your nature snarls, yaps, barks for nothing, really, except that pain be absent from the body and mind enjoy delight, with fear dispelled, anxiety gone."

It is up to Job to choose the way he will surrender to his whirlwind. He has already recognized God in it. But he also knows that the presence of God does not always mean comfort and peace. Will he now be dragged down by the whirlwind or be lifted up to heaven? The resolution of his situation will depend on it. His world, that of his friends, the whole of nature must yield to the voice of the whirlwind. But is Job strong enough to hear it? Is he willing enough to seek the message contained in it?

Today's whirlwind is both personal and collective. Where does one start the search for the divine? How much can one gain from the advice and teaching of friends, religious leaders, professors, and writers? Our propensity to distort the essential and emphasize the immediate has given birth to multitudes of perspectives that never allow a holistic view of the kingdom.

Job knew his whirlwind. Do we recognize and know ours? Can we name the whirlwind from which God might choose to speak to us? In the case of Job, it was worth God's determination to break his silence and to intervene in a desperate situation. Are our whirlwinds sufficiently important for God to enter them and force us to listen to him and to argue with him? We have argued so much with each other that there seems to be no room for God to enter the debate. On the stage of religious history, chaos has taken us farther and farther away from each other and from a common language. Like the friends of Job, and especially Elihu, we lose our spiritual sharpness to the point of not even surmising that our beliefs and expectations may no longer be in tune with the original creative purpose. As in Job's case, God may choose to address us out of a whirlwind beyond our grasp and force us to hear a voice totally different from what we have grown accustomed to in our cherished traditions. All we can do is pray that when the message comes to us, we shall have a faith strong enough to hear it and accept it even if we find ourselves alone in the struggle.

MEDITATION 55.

"Where were you when I laid the foundation of the earth?" (Job 38:4)

Out of the whirlwind God answered Job with a question which served as a gentle reminder of his relative insignificance in the process of creation. He was not destined to share the secrets through which things came into being. The world was before we were and shall remain when we are no more. In a way, God rebukes Job for trying to find an answer to his situation as though he were important.

Where were we when God was creating? We were in his mind as an extension of his creative urge. Creation remains a divine act, and the ages of human history and the wisdom they contain will never reveal to us the primordial and original blueprint. All we know is that the world contains flaws that even God is not eager to correct. Is Job then so wrong in trying to ascertain whether God can vindicate what seems contrary to his nature?

When we were not yet, the world appeared good, and "all the sons of God shouted for joy." How ironic that to know that goodness, Job must journey through the valley of suffering and destitution. While he contemplates his abject misery, the universe of God's creation—all the stars and heavenly bodies—continue to function around him according to principles of perfection. Thus, Job's painful realization that there is no relation between that perfection and life on earth. Job was reminded that his plight does not come from personal misfortune but from the fundamental ignorance of the mysteries of creation. Destined to live in a world we will never understand, we are also deprived of the right to complain.

. . . .

We praise our ability to discover the workings of God's creation. But it is equally necessary to be conscious of the limits we shall never be allowed to cross. We must learn how to be thankful for the things we know as well as for the things we do not know, for the things God has chosen to reveal to us and for those he must keep hidden from us, for the things that are bound to temporality and for those that will cross over to eternity. Some mysteries are revealed to us, others are kept secret. This should lead neither to arrogance nor to discouragement. Creation contains more mysteries than we can comprehend. This is not vanity, but a reminder that our minds and hearts never cease to wonder at the greatness of the divine architect.

The mystery of the unknown has shaped our relationship to God, nature, and the self. We do not understand the universal purpose of being. We must partake of that which is foreign to us and transform our feeling of estrangement into a vision of hope, however little it may ever be realized.

There shall always be a sober reminder that we cannot know all of what could be known. This fact will ensure a perpetual striving toward the unreachable. To know more about our human condition is also to discover more about God's majesty. Wisdom helps us distinguish between arrogance and humility.

Present with God at the beginning of time was wisdom as described in a personified form in the Book of Proverbs: "When he established the heavens, I was there, when he drew a circle on the face of the deep, when he made firm the skies above, when he established the fountains of the deep, when he assigned to the sea its limit, so that the waters might not transgress his command, when

. . . .

he marked out the foundations of the earth, then I was beside him, like a master workman; and I was daily his delight, rejoicing before him always, rejoicing in his inhabited world and delighting in the sons of men." Perhaps this was a language Job could understand, for only in our search for divine wisdom can we come closer to beholding some of God's majesty. It is through that share of wisdom, through the spark of the *logos* in every one of us that we were in God's mind from the beginning, sharing before we could know it in a divine purpose that persists beyond suffering and revolt.

It is only at the edge of infinity, with the consciousness that we appear in the cosmos as incomplete beings in an unfinished universe, that the question of where we were when God laid the foundation of the world becomes relevant. The answer to it, however, remains elusive. Boundaries within which we are trapped persist in spite of our toils. Some great mysteries of life may be within our surmise, but out of our reach. Knowledge cannot dispel chaos, for nothing that is done under the sun is marked by coherence and harmony. We persist in the search for unity, knowing that we shall wander from possibility to possibility, finding satisfaction for only a brief time in a very limited area. God keeps hidden from us many mysteries of life while endowing us with the gift of resisting ignorance.

But for now Job is much too aware of the fact that he has become a disturbing presence in God's cosmos. It is in his search that he rises far above those who never dare question God. T. S. Eliot summarizes the feeling in his poetry: "And indeed there will be a time to wonder, 'Do I dare?' and 'Do I dare?' Time to turn back and descend the stair, with a bald spot in the middle of my hair. . . . Do I dare disturb the universe." In the most inscrutable of ways, Job was there from the beginning, and he is there now, with everyone of us, in the eternal purpose of God, both obstacle and joy. And he knew, like many of us, that the only way to God is through a relentless striving to overcome the obstacles separating us from him.

It does not seem to have been God's concern to ensure our comfort on this planet. Rather, we are called upon to learn what we can and to accept the inscrutable mysteries. We cannot understand how our tenuous hold on life connects with God's purpose. It is for us to imagine, and perhaps create, eternal modes of knowing within the finitude of time. Job couldn't answer the question as to whether he was there at creation, nor could we. But now we are here, and God's creation must contain us whether or not we know and understand any universal scheme.

"Where were you when I laid the foundation of the earth?" Who but God could ask—and answer—such a question?

MEDITATION 56.

"Will you even put me in the wrong? Will you condemn me that you may be justified?" (Job 40:8)

hy did Job fail to observe what is obvious in creation? Perhaps because it is not so obvious. The divine litany of human failures leads Job to realize that being within God's creation does not ensure our understanding of it. If there is a final design in nature, it escapes our scrutiny, hence, the temptation to assign the source of disorder to God.

For a long time Job thrashed out his perplexing situation with his friends. In spite of his persuasiveness, he did not win many arguments. Fatigue sets in when our endeavors end in futility. Job could have compiled the thoughts and debates of his friends and written volumes of theology. In fact, he is overwhelmed by their intelligence and cogency, though they cannot help him. In the end, he seeks a last vindication with God. But instead of a bold discourse, we are invited to hear his confession of humility: "Behold, I am of small account; what shall I answer thee?"

"Come, let us reason together." Such were the words attributed by Isaiah to God in the midst of a debate on the nature of sin. Even in the darkest moments there is room for a dialogue with God. Job is exhausted and ready to abandon the fight, an outcome God must avoid. After all, God has made his purpose depend on the virtues of Job. Not without some irony, God has allowed his perfection to be contingent on the righteousness of a human being.

. . . .

In the perils of life the religion of Job has undergone an important process of purification and refinement. He searched for his place in a puzzling world. He refused to be blinded by events and arguments that had a logical explanation but that could not lead to the truth he was pursuing. He learned what many of us are incapable of accepting, namely that winning arguments does not automatically bring us closer to the truth.

The voice out of the whirlwind persists in Job's consciousness. In fact, it constitutes the apex of the debate, the culminating point of all reflection, the insight into the purest form of religion available to us. In the intimate presence of God, our questions lose their intensity and importance. All along Job was absorbed in a search that led him to question why the innocent suffer and why the wicked prosper. Had he reached a satisfactory explanation, he might have solved his own dilemma. But it was not meant to be, and he had to learn in humility that he could not be the sole master of his destiny or the architect of his redemption.

The inclination to attribute to God wrong intentions comes from a rational investigation of nature's behavior. A world of tragic events and spiritual turmoil is also a world devoid of ultimate perfection. At least, it so appeared to Job who could not reconcile divine goodness and human suffering.

Interestingly, God is provoked to defend himself against this very thought. When the divine voice comes out of the whirlwind again, God establishes the context in which the dialogue can continue: "Shall a faultfinder contend with the Almighty?" If Job wishes to continue his argument with God, he will have to answer for it. In fact God anticipates Job's approach and moves directly

. . . .

into the center of contention: "Will you even put me in the wrong? Will you condemn me that you may be justified?" Was this Job's purpose? Even in his most rebellious moments, when everything pointed to his right to reject God, he never ceased to proclaim the Lord's wisdom and majesty.

God did not owe Job such a long explanation of how his creation came to be and of how it is proceeding now. Has God found in Job a greater debater than he expected? Have we now reached, as Jung suggests, the unthinkable limits where the creature could slip into higher forms of perception than the creator? Has God pushed the wager too far with Job and is now placed in the position of defending his behavior against the logical responses of Job?

Two worlds are locked in endless conflict. Does the justification of the one demand the condemnation of the other? In a world torn apart by forces of evil, there can be no self-evident praise of a benevolent creator. Job has now found a way to deal with those evil forces, but little does he know that they are not distinct from divine will, that, in his case, they are the result of a wager God must win. Suffering has opened a door through which Job peers into the divine. There, on the basis of pure rationality, God may stand condemned, unable to master the forces he may have unleashed on the world. Thus it is imperative that God establish his superiority even in a world which is marked by forces antagonistic to his purpose.

"Will you put me in the wrong? Will you condemn me that you can be justified?" What kind of answer could Job propose to such a challenge? What kind of response could anyone formulate in times of distress when all appears beyond understanding and endurance? It is a normal reaction for us to seek justification, even when wrong. But few would dare put God in the wrong. Job, more than anybody else, would have had the right to do so. But through all his anguish and anxiety he did not sin. God knew Job's answer to his question. Had he not, the wager would have never taken place, and the question would have remained eternally irrelevant.

Job did not choose to participate in a drama in which he was cast as an innocent victim who was not supposed to rise to such a high level of consciousness. But there he is, and God must allow for the determination of some of us to penetrate the meaning of the stage on which our lives evolve, even if it implies finding fault with the work of a perfect creator.

MEDITATION 57.

Behemoth and Leviathan. (Job 40:15; 41:1)

ar greater threats to God's creation than the sons of God are Behemoth and Leviathan, two mythological monsters opposed to God's purpose in creation. They are the product of chaos. They belong to the original abyss as it existed before the divine *logos* called it into order. Their intent is rudimentary and simple: fight for the return of chaos within which they do not feel threatened.

The forces of evil symbolized by Behemoth and Leviathan can and will be unleashed on the world, and every participant in creation will feel the wounds inflicted by the presence of that which opposes God and leaves life unfulfilled. But Job must know that nothing ever happens without God's rule and consent, even when it is accompanied by a curse we cannot explain. God made what opposes him, and therefore it is not separate from him: "Behold, Behemoth, which I made as I made you." Did God expect Job to oppose him as much as Behemoth did, simply because they both belong to the same order of things? How much of the Behemoth and the Leviathan is there in every one of us even when our yearning is to worship God with all our heart and strength?

Both Leviathan and Behemoth belong to a divine comedy whose meaning we cannot penetrate. We are left with surmises of religious visions and images that have disappeared with those who created them in ancient times. The Psalmist occasionally took a lighter approach to the existence of Leviathan and suggested that God created him for his amusement: "There go the ships and Leviathan which thou didst form to sport in it" (or, "Leviathan which you made to amuse you").

But the days of Leviathan are numbered. His destruction must precede final salvation. Again the psalmist tries to put things in the right perspective: "Yet God my King is from old, working salvation in the midst of the earth . . . Thou didst crush the head of Leviathan, thou didst give him as food for the creatures of the wilderness." The prophetic voice of Isaiah is even more definite. No eschatological redemption can leave room for what is contrary to God: "In that day the Lord with his hard and great and strong sword will punish Leviathan the fleeing serpent, Leviathan the twisting serpent, and he will slay the dragon which is in the sea." For the time being, however, Job is left to wonder why there is such a delay in divine vengeance and in the vindication of the innocent.

Order and chaos represent two different aspects of the same reality, the former winning over the latter without annihilating it. Behemoth and Leviathan will bring havoc on humankind until the end of time, before being defeated in a final clash with God. But for now, chaos cannot be differentiated from order. Thus, God must remind Job that, although it is not evident, everything is under divine control.

We may wonder, like Job, about the existence of Behemoth and Leviathan. If God created them, for what purpose did he do so? Certainly not just to amuse himself. What is it that requires the divinity to know both good and evil? That question must remain a mystery to us and certainly could not provide much comfort to Job. Chaos and evil are present as integral parts of creation.

. . . .

Conflict must persist as the source of our yearning for redemption. Should one welcome Behemoth and Leviathan, or fight them? We probably can do neither successfully, since God alone holds those decisions in his hands.

In poetic form, Job is reminded of the strength and majesty of divinely created monsters. They become the mirrors of God's rule of the world. To recognize them is also to experience the awe of divine presence. Somehow Job failed to know this, for it could not be a part of his view of God's relationship to the world. That we should find God through what is contrary to him does not make a great deal of sense to us either. Yet, we should have learned from experience that there is hardly any other way to remain on the path to redemption.

Behemoth and Job are parts of the same creative process, made for the same purpose, having both existed in God's mind from all eternity. Why, then, has Job become so unhappy and so unperceiving of God's universal plan? There is no path leading back to God but the one where we meet Behemoth and Leviathan.

MEDITATION 58.

"Therefore I have uttered what I did not understand, things too wonderful for me, which I did not know." (Job 42:3)

Job's epilogue—the final words of a traveler who experienced so many mysteries without knowing what they meant, while feeling within himself the wonders of the journey. Now Job realizes that meaning does not always come from understanding. What a lesson for our scientific and technological world! We have grown accustomed to place value only on that which can be proven or explained. Oscar Wilde suggested that what can be proven is not worth proving. How do we reach into the mysteries which refuse to be subjected to our principles of verification?

Job does not answer this. Sometimes, when we are drawn into the mysteries of creation, it is enough to marvel at life, even when we can explain very little of it. There is a knowledge which is self-sufficient, a natural possession of the soul. We must cultivate it, even when it contradicts all the principles and canons of traditional scholarship.

Job is overwhelmed, not because he penetrated some of the divine secrets, but because those secrets were part of his being even when everything conspired to hide them from him. Who will ever know how much of divine essence is already within us? That knowledge does not come from our participation in the world of education, however important that world is. It is born and grows in solitariness; it is essentially religious; it belongs to a close contact with the God who created us.

. . . .

Every now and then we stand in need of reassurance while we seek the meaning and purpose of our existence. There is so much more to life than what we can know and say about it at any given time. We carry within us treasures that we are not fully aware of and that we fail to nurture properly. The creator who put those treasures in us does not ensure that we can know them fully. Our daily preoccupations, our temporality, our anxieties, and sometimes even our joys stand in the way of our communion with God.

When our earthly pilgrimage comes to its end, how much of life will we have missed? How much of it have previous generations taken to their graves? We are destined to recover that which from eternity belonged to us, never knowing at what point of the journey we are nor how far we will be allowed to proceed. In the meantime we, too, utter what we do not understand, things too wonderful for us to know. While some of those divine gifts are buried in our sinful selves, the world continues on its path of suffering, conflicts, wars, anger, and pretensions to a goodness we are never able to implement.

Our life on earth is indeed precarious. We strive to uncover more and more of the intellectual and spiritual riches within our reach. Yet even our moral progress often leads to greater errors. It is by virtue of our moral endowments that we become capable of evil. The more deeply Job penetrated into the inscrutability of divine action, the more he rebelled and argued with God, and the more he felt estranged from what he wished his essential being to be.

Faith cannot solve the greatest paradox, namely that our redemption rests more on what cannot be revealed to us than on what we can know. It is only through faith that we can commit our lives to a divine

. . . .

compassion of which we know only the surface. Our hope resides in that which is not yet. In his relationship to his disciples, Christ felt the discrepancy between what he wanted to reveal to them and what they were capable of receiving: "I have yet many things to say to you, but you cannot bear them now." Eternity alone will last long enough for us to know and to become what God had intended for us to be from the beginning.

I have often wondered what the life of the people of God would be if, instead of debating our dogmas and tenets, we found ourselves immersed in thought and prayer, in search for what is not yet ours. As long as Job and his friends were locked into endless arguments trying to prove all kinds of situations, no solution was in sight. Not that those debates were fruitless or irrelevant. They belonged to the unavoidable questions of life. But they could not bring relief to the absurdity of the moment. It was only when the mind and heart of Job were turned toward wonders of the not yet known, that he was overwhelmed by a divine presence. He had again learned the simple yet difficult lesson, namely that God is always in the beyond of everything we know, feel, believe, and profess.

Job does not carry with him the memory of his plight. Isolated from the wider purpose of God, his suffering would remain absurd. But in the perspective of eternity, it opens up doors for him he could never have found on his own. It is the end of the journey which enlightens every step of it, whether or not it made sense.

Are we too eager to make sure that everything in life makes sense? Is that not imposing our views and prejudices on a reality that, in fact, begs for more than we can comprehend? But then, Job generates a strange feeling in us. On the one hand, he lets us know that there is more

. . . .

to life than what we have experienced. On the other hand, we may remain frustrated at the thought that the true meaning of life may not be disclosed to us until we reach the end of it. If then.

"Therefore I have uttered what I did not understand, things too wonderful for me, which I did not know." What a wonderful summary of both our greatness and our limitations, our knowledge and our faith, our fellowship with the Lord and our aspirations to live in a closer communion with him, our burden of temporality and our hope of eternity, our threatened earthly existence and our yearning for immortality!

. . . .

MEDITATION 59.

The Perils of Friendship. (Job 42:7–9)

he friends of Job failed to bring comfort to him, but they were genuine friends who spent countless hours with a companion they could not abandon to his misery. Their wisdom was the product of long years of reflection and analysis, but it could not meet God's standards. They marvelled at the fact that Job's suffering would not diminish his resolve to pursue with passion a freedom and a determination he refused to surrender. The counsels of his friends, though offered in a spirit of genuine friendship, appeared to him as false consolation which faded into the unacceptable. Was Job fair? Was God fair?

The affirmation of Seneca that friendship "is a sovereign antidote against all calamities, even against the fear of death" has received universal acclaim. But it does not verify itself in the case of Job. His friends shunned no trouble in their quest to serve as new eyes, new hearts, and new tongues as he walked the path of turmoil and uncertainty. They were partners in a set of circumstances that eluded explanation. Were Job's friends guilty of misconduct because they pursued a search that was beyond their ability? Should not that be credited to them as a mark of intelligence and perseverance?

Good will and wisdom do not always achieve their intended goal. Far from soothing his grief, the friends of Job irritated him. We wonder at what else they could have done or said. The tears of Job's friends, their distressed silence for a whole week, their words, and all other expressions of compassion represent what anyone of us would have done in similar circumstances. Would Peter, Augustine, Kierkegaard, or any other great religious personality have been able to bring better comfort to Job than Eliphaz, Zophar, and Bildad? Could anyone know what constitutes our supreme tribunal in our quest for truth? Is there a personal aspect to our destiny that escapes the purview of everybody else? The sharing of our convictions, as virtuous and as noble as they can appear to us, does not always put us right with our friends.

Would Job have fared better had he had no friends? That is the impression we get at the end of the story. The anger of God against Job's friends strikes us as profound divine injustice. If Job was not meant to be comforted, why put friends on his path?

Cicero spoke of friendship as a "second self" and defined it as "nothing else but an agreement in all things, divine and human, combined with good will and affection; I am inclined to think," he added, "that with the exception of wisdom nothing better than this has been given to man by the immortal gods." From a human point of view, no one could reproach the friends of Job. From a divine point of view, they stand accused of lacking the wisdom that could have mediated comfort to Job.

At the end of the story, we are led to believe that Job did not really want the consolation of his friends. Their explanations and answers could not fit anywhere in his tormented quest for the behavior of a God he thought he understood but could no longer comprehend. It was impossible to help him because the divine nature of the wager did not allow it. But could anyone blame his friends for not perceiving that? In a long speech in which Job voiced his complaints against divine hostility, he

. . . .

reproached God for purposefully misleading his friends: "Since thou hast closed their minds to understanding, therefore thou wilt not let them triumph."

How much friendship could we share with anybody if we had to make sure that it is of the purest form and perfect? Is friendship not, after all, a sharing of everything, including our flaws and liabilities? Why should God meet good will with anger? Job was not guiltless either. If it is true that in some instances his friends lacked wisdom, so did he. The turmoil Job and his friends were thrown into was not of human making, but had to be solved on the basis of human wisdom. Now the verdict is in. Job was right, his friends wrong. Are we to believe that right and wrong are so clearly delineated that they can be totally on one side or the other?

True, one of the worst feelings we can experience is to have been a bad friend, or a powerless friend, to someone in need. But a friendship remains a friendship, a noble gesture in a chaotic world. Should some higher power decree that we must be punished for not being able to provide the right kind of friendship, it remains a fact that that is better than never to have been a friend to anyone. Friendship must be accepted for what it is, even when it differs from what we expect.

When I was a young coal miner, one of my friends was stricken with a severe case of black lung disease. Soon his situation deteriorated into life-threatening complications. I visited him regularly at the hospital, trying to provide some acts of kindness that might alleviate his suffering. For a long time after his death, I was still troubled by the thought that there could have been many more gestures of compassion on my part. Guilt accompanies us when we are overwhelmed by the realization

. . . .

that our friendship for the suffering was incomplete and insufficient. Perhaps it is the friends of Job who should have been consoled after they discovered how inadequate they had been in their duties to a friend.

Now, as a final act, Job will have to pray for the forgiveness of his friends, the only prayer God is willing to hear. When we accept to atone for the sins of friends, we come closer to God than in any other circumstance. "No longer do I call you servants . . . but I have called you friends," said Jesus to his disciples. He knew of the risks and disappointments involved in such a move.

One of the most stirring and noble episodes of the Old Testament takes place after the people in the wilderness make a golden calf under the leadership of their spiritual mentor, Aaron. Full of grief, Moses goes back to the mountain to plead with God and says, "But now, if thou wilt forgive their sin—and if not, blot me, I pray thee, out of thy book which thou hast written." There is little doubt that we have here the highest level of sacrifice in the name of friendship, namely to be willing to forfeit one's salvation for others in the hope that it be extended to them despite their errors and undeserving natures.

Job must have the last word. His friends could not be right because they were not part of the wager. They had to interpret a situation they were not privileged to understand, so they could not deal with the core of the matter. Whatever they said was based on the conviction that they mediated God's wisdom to Job. But they did it in such a legalistic way and with such traditional religious clichés that they failed to perceive the sense of tragedy surrounding the specific situation Job found himself in

. . . .

and which could not be resolved on a purely rational plane.

Against their knowledge and will, Job's friends were locked in a framework of speech and feeling that could not properly address the needs of their companion in his new and baffling situation. As a rule we do not understand our friends in their deeply personal circumstances. At best, we can compare our thoughts and feelings to theirs, hoping that we have gained the right insight into their predicaments. Perhaps the most discouraging sense of being at an impasse came from the fact that Job himself could not properly estimate and analyze a new mode of thought and belief which was the product of unexpected and incomprehensible events ruling his life. At points Job must have appeared to himself as something else than what he could have expected in life. To know oneself truly in all conditions of life may not be an achievable goal. It may not have been for Job or for his friends.

Under other circumstances, all the speeches of Job's friends would have been acceptable, but not when God himself allowed confusion to be directed at a person he had chosen to be the representative of a mystery beyond traditional events. We do not know whether Job and his friends remained on good terms, but without their multiple contacts, the whole story of Job would have remained meaningless. That is sufficient vindication.

MEDITATION 60.

Epilogue: The New Job (Job 42:10–17)

appy are those who can find their spiritual home at the end of the journey!

With a resilience unavailable to most of us, Job overcame physical and spiritual obstacles. Like a survivor of the household of Noah on the ark, he could contemplate the reappearance of a lost world which had been engulfed in the destructive forces of purification and cleansing. The memories of past times still echoed in a distant void now replaced by a new spiritual reality. In many ways the new world resembled the old one, but its content was different. Divine anger had subsided. Some leviathans disappeared, others continued to claim their place of prominence. Creative purpose still failed to be obvious, and the quest will persist forever, leading either to anxiety or faith.

A reality in turmoil threatens our longing for inner peace. The journey of Job, as well as of humankind, has not ended. On occasion it can be rewarding. But most often we find ourselves as lonely travelers deprived of maps which could identify our destination in a divine plan never totally clear to us. One cannot reach home without crossing the infinite spaces of a universe in suffering.

Job's mosaic of fragments could find its meaning only within the eternal circle of divine compassion, under the rainbow of old and new covenants that have guided God's people from the days of Noah to the revelation of John at Patmos. Like Job, we come to the door of eternity battered but not defeated. Like him, we finally enter the time of healing.

. . . .

In the end, Job has twice as much as before. He has also been made the recipient of a long and happy life. But this new Job seems different from the one who just proclaimed, "Now my eye sees thee; therefore I despise myself, and repent in dust and ashes."

The Book of Job may have gained in depth and virtue without the perplexing epilogue in which divine blessings are material. Job is no longer involved in an analysis of all sides of life, including terror. He has become a passive recipient of material possessions, showered on him.

Where is the Job with whom we journeyed through the mysterious apprehensions of life? That Job was closer to us and to every one who has experienced the blows of fate and the devastations of life. Few encounter the kind of corrective Job was privileged to receive.

Perhaps we should not be the recipients of material blessings if we are to nurture the quest for what lies beyond our understanding. The Job at the end of the story no longer has anything to teach us. He has ceased to represent humankind in its suffering, in its doubts, in its anxieties, in its mystery.

So why does the book end the way it does? Is it in the name of divine fair play? Is it to reward a unique person? Or is it to show that in a broken world the system of rewards and punishments grinds to its end, bitter for some, sweet for others? From a human point of view, the end of the story is reassuring—it gives us hope. From a realistic point of view, it is tragically misleading. One simply cannot expect to be in Job's camp. If possessing material goods is the reward of virtue, then we must look for some other kind of virtue more akin to that of Socrates or Spinoza.

But then again, the Book of Job may be regarded as a lengthy metaphor of the *apokatastasis tôn pantôn*, the

. . . .

restoration of all things to God's initial purpose. God's creation cannot remain forever threatened and unfinished. Some day we shall receive far more than what we have, albeit in spiritual and not material rewards, in divine blessings against which God's adversary will have no power, in virtues that will be worth taking with us into eternity.

For the time being, it suffices to know that Satan has disappeared from the picture and that we have progressively moved to the victory over the forces of evil. In that sense, Job embodies all of humanity again. God's providence does not fail the world. Righteousness finds its vindication. Justice and mercy prevail.

There was a man in the land of Uz, a servant of God chosen to become the mirror reflecting the experience of countless faithful pilgrims in search of an explanation to inscrutable mysteries in an existence replete with tragedy and suffering. The Book of Job was not meant to alter our journey through life, but to make it more meaningful.

As companions of Job, searching for our assigned destiny through the perils of life, we come to know ourselves as part of a divine purpose far greater than what we expected. Like Job, we come back to our beginnings, sometimes depleted, rebellious and frustrated, and sometimes enriched and thankful.

It belongs to us, as we contemplate life in both its temporal and eternal dimensions, to pass judgment on our expectations and to define our place among the living. And when suffering and despair fill our lives, we must find the strength to avail ourselves of the divine gifts through which we can create our personal reasons to live a life which can transcend our immediate limitations. So we

. . . .

turn again to the example of Job. It may not always bring us comfort, but it brings us closer to the truth.

Survivors of recent holocausts, be they from Nazi concentration camps or from places such as Hiroshima, could have written their own "Book of Job." Even on a more humane level, some of us can recall parts of our journey through the desolation of life and through the cruelty of fate. We keep in our memory the pain of unanswered pleas, the loss of loved ones, the bewilderment at human injustice, the sense of futility about prayers which were of no avail, and still question the nature of God's compassion when he leaves us hurting and when we are overcome by the feeling of isolation and loneliness.

The poetic beauty and poignancy of the Book of Job requires a denouement equal only to the majesty of God. Job is restored to a life of blessings, all of them greater than he could have ever expected. But can he take us with him to the empyrean he himself discovered only after a long journey into the night of desolation?

The *Ancient of Days* is still wielding his compass of perfect forms, while natural disasters, famines, wars, misery, illness, death, and suffering of all kinds continue to torment our world. We may have to search for a message that remains unwritten and unutterable in clear words. Job, who for a time stood as the most destitute person among the living, speaks the message again, a *logos* shared by the prophets and surpassed only in Christ.

In humility, we acknowledge the fact that we do not know the "why" of so many things and events. In faith we accept the wisdom of a God who gives and takes away. In hope we refuse to give despair the final word.

. . . .

When, at the end of our earthly pilgrimage, we take our bread and our wine to the altar of eternity in remembrance of the ultimate suffering which brought redemption to our world, we may finally understand why the whole earth received its purpose from the great heroes of faith who would not let the creative spirit die. And we may praise God for the things we learned from the story of Job, for the forces of life that continue to rise even after our bodily strength vanishes, for all the diverse elements which, in spite of their temporary absurdity, converge toward a divine unity beyond our surmise. Like Job we may have witnessed days which brought us success or failure. We may have seen the power of life surge in us or the fear of death diminish our resolve. We may have found our own ash pit where every hope dissolves into nothingness until we too learn how to gather up in our arms the fragments of broken lives and implore the Lord to make us whole again and mediate that wholeness to the world around us.

In suffering, we discover that we are both children of heaven and sons and daughters of the earth, that part of us suffers a continuous process of death while our spirits rise to new apprehensions of the realm of redemption. And then we may offer a silent prayer of gratitude to God when we penetrate the most ineffable mystery of all, namely that for all eternity we were in God and with God, precious elements in a purpose too great for us to comprehend.

As we break the bread and drink the cup, we too become the suffering presence of God in the world, for it is in the body of Christ that the Jobs of all generations meet. Some day the kingdom will come in its full force as the result of the sufferings of God's servants. And some day, the hand of the Redeemer will wipe away the last

. . . .

tears from our eyes, as we shall pass into the final communion with God and live in the presence of the One who is so much greater than anything we could conceive of through our faith, through our love, and through our hope.

ABOUT THE AUTHOR

Paul Ciholas was born the son of a minister in a small French village in 1930. As a boy, Ciholas assisted his father during World War II in ministering to Russian prisoners whom the Nazis held in his village. After the war, he labored in the coal mines of Northern France.

Ciholas went on to earn degrees from the University of Paris and the International Theological Seminary, culminating with a Ph.D. in Philosophical Theology from the University of Strasbourg. He then pastored Baptist churches in France. After moving to the United States, he served as an interim pastor at Briggs Memorial Baptist Church in Washington, D.C., where he once opened the U.S. Senate session with prayer. Later, Ciholas taught religion at universities in North Carolina and Kentucky, taking early retirement in 1991 to pursue research and writing.

At this writing, he has several works in progress regarding subjects as diverse as Greek philosophers, New Testament characters, and meditations on Easter. His international background, his eye-witness experiences of the suffering caused by Hitler, and his perceptive intellect make him uniquely qualified to interpret the themes that affect us so profoundly from the Book of Job.

Consider my servant Job : me
50617